TRUCK THIS

FOR A LIVING

Tales of a UK Lorry Driver

By Gary Mottram

Dedicated to truckers, lorry drivers, multi-drop van drivers and the men and women that work, and live, on the roads around the world

TRUCK THIS FOR A LIVING

The wind was howling on the quayside, the rain had been lashing down for the last 5 hours. I was soaked through to the skin; we all were, despite our heavy-duty waterproof jackets and trousers. Our shift started at 6pm the night before, a Saturday, and it was rapidly approaching 5am on Sunday morning, but we were still nowhere near finishing. The boat we were unloading, bobbing frantically in the water beside us, still had another 6 loads to discharge, each load destined for a yard 1 mile up the road. Nearly every load had been 7 small offshore containers; 15 ratchet straps per journey.

It was a struggle to throw the straps over the load, which was standing around 13ft high, the wind whipping them back down to the ground as soon as you let go. Over the noise of the crane I heard my phone ring so headed for the peace of my cab to answer it;

"You know the boat that came into the harbour last night?" said the voice from operations echoing from the stillness of a cosy, warm office.

"Yes, the boat you said you weren't going to start

unloading until 8am, when the dayshift trucks started their shift?"

"That's the one" came the reply "Well, I've decided that we are going to continue straight on after this boat is finished so I'll need 6 trucks on that"

"Bloody hell", I protested, "You know we knock off at 6, how am I supposed to get drivers out with that short notice?"

"Not my problem" came the distant reply.

There was nothing else for it but to start making some phone calls.....

LET'S GO BACK A FEW YEARS...

I have always wanted to drive trucks.

From an early age I was obsessed. My uncle was a long-distance lorry driver and I spent many happy hours playing in the yard where he kept his truck. It was great just being around these huge beasts. Sadly, I never got to ride in his cab, thanks to my parents. He once offered to take me on a run from the south coast to Birmingham but, because it was a school day, my parents wouldn't allow me to go. I firmly believe I would have learned more about life in that one day than I would in a whole term at school. Instead, I had to make do with watching from a distance. I used to love the local carnival parade. I wasn't remotely interested in the floats, choosing instead to watch how the lorries moved, to feel the heat from them, to hear the loud engine noise and the hiss of air brakes, to smell the diesel fumes. I loved all the spotlights and chrome, the tassels and curtains in the comfy looking cabs. Above all, I loved to imagine what it must be like to sit up that high and look out of that huge windscreen.

As I got older and started driving, it was still at the

back of my mind as being something I would like to do. The more I thought about it, the scarier it became and I knew I probably never would. I had seen trucks shunting around and trying to reverse into stupidly small entrances, I'd seen trucks on their side on roundabouts, I'd seen jack-knifed trucks on the motorway, I'd read about drivers being beaten up or kidnapped for their precious load and decided anything that could happen, probably would.

Still, I loved being stuck on the motorway surrounded by noisy trucks, checking all the trucker paraphernalia in the windscreen, reading all the company names and locations on the cab door, bringing to mind the barges and narrow boats that once plied their own trade up and down the canals of this country, the motorways of old (albeit at a speed of 5 miles per hour), adorned with colourful paintwork and signwriting, carrying raw materials to all the major towns and cities, and back again, with the finished product for export to some far off land.

IN THE BEGINNING

I left school aged 16 after getting average exam grades. It wasn't that I was unintelligent, but just got easily distracted. 'Must do better' was on pretty much every report I took home from age 13 to 16. I flirted with many career choices including mechanic, banker, policeman, Royal Marine, music shop owner and rock star (this one actually kept my mind off school and the future for a good few years and still does, if I'm truthful).

So, how the hell did I end up making musical instruments for 12 years? Well, I have always been interested in music, playing in brass bands and orchestras as a young man, not to mention numerous rock/punk/metal bands as an adult. So when I saw an advert in the local paper for a trainee musical instrument maker, I had to enquire. I was currently 2 months into a 'Business Studies' college course but it was very boring and, unknown to my parents, I had been bunking off for the best part of a month.

Two weeks later I started as a trainee woodwind musical instrument maker, learning lots of new skills. These skills would actually be useless as this company is the only large woodwind instrument makers in the UK. Still, it didn't pay too bad and was better than working at Tesco. It also gave me some direction for the future rather than leaving college with a useless qualification that I would probably never use and I would still be no nearer to knowing what I wanted to do with my life.

I stuck with this job for 9 years until I felt I needed to move on. I was by now 25, my father had recently died, and I just had the feeling I needed to move out of the south and live somewhere different. The firm had a few 'out-workers' that used to turn up once a month to bring their finished instruments, get paid, and take away new components to be made into more instruments. They essentially worked on a self-employed basis from home. This seemed like heaven to me. How great would it be to be your own boss, to not have to get up for work every day and not to have to put up with self-important supervisors and co-workers that, at times, could drive you round the bend? After a lot of organisation from my boss, and after selling my home in Hampshire, I was moving north to Yorkshire. I had wanted to move away for a while and this place seemed as good as anywhere. Looking back, I think I needed to get away from the snobbery of the south, and it did me a lot of good to get out of my comfort zone and live somewhere gritty.

I was self-employed for 4 years and it was as great as I had imagined. In that time, I travelled extensively for both business and pleasure, and the old driving bug returned.

I was speaking to a lad one day on the phone, after he replied to one of my (many) 'musicians wanted' adverts. This is a whole other book so I won't go into detail, but he said he currently lived in Bristol but would happily move to Yorkshire to be in the right band. I asked him what he would do for a job and he replied that he would find an agency job as a van driver. The band didn't work out, but this bit of information proved to be very useful as I never thought it would be that easy to start driving for a living. Admittedly, I hadn't looked into it, but the seed was sown that day and remained in the back of my mind for when I would need it. Over the next few months I started checking out some of the agencies in my area to see what they had available and even signed up with one agency but never actually worked for them as they wanted to take me on for a long term contract and, due to being self-employed, I didn't have the time to do both jobs.

Around this time, I replied to an advert in the local paper looking for a part-time delivery driver. I got the job and was soon delivering pies and sausage rolls in the early morning to 8 bakers in and around Manchester. It was quite enjoyable and the £70 a week came in very handy. I lasted for a few months until one morning when I got a puncture on the M62. I was on my way back to drop the van off in Halifax when I felt the steering go heavy and the vehicle was pulling to the left. I managed to wrestle the vehicle into Birch services and discovered the nearside front tyre was flat. On closer inspection, the tyre was actually worn through to the steel, causing the tyre to deflate. Once I had changed the tyre, I took it back to the yard and told the boss. He just laughed and said "We got our money's worth out of that tyre". I took offence to this and told him where he could stick his job.

It was also a valuable lesson:

ALWAYS CHECK YOUR VEHICLE BEFORE DRIVING IT!

A while later, I moved house to Nottingham. Approximately a month after moving in, I 'phoned to see if my next batch of instruments were ready for collection. I soldered the keywork together and fitted it to the instrument, so needed someone 'down south' to turn the wooden body of the instruments and drill the sound holes so I could take them away and do my bit to them. I also wanted to know if my boss would be around to give me my monthly pay cheque. He was often away on business or holiday and would happily leave a cheque for me if he wasn't about. On this occasion, the voice at the end of the 'phone was pale and distant and, after a deathly silence, told me he would call me back in a minute. I waited for what seemed like an eternity until the telephone rang. My boss announced that they would no longer need my services, they would pay me for the work already done, but that was it. The call lasted no longer than a couple of minutes and, in that short time, my world came crashing down. I was flabbergasted. My legs turned to jelly and I couldn't stand. I always knew this was a possibility as I was self-employed, it's one of the risks, but the shock of it actually happening was unbelievable. 13 years of my life I had done the same job, here I was now with no qualifications, no experience of doing anything else (my paper round and the tomato picking job I had when I left school didn't count) and no idea what I was going to do. I hated living in Nottingham, I found it a depressing place, and didn't want my daughter to grow up there (it was the gun capital of Britain at the time, above Brixton and Moss Side).

I had to think of a way to get some money together, pay the rent, and start thinking about moving somewhere different.

Well, there was one idea........

I had always remembered the telephone conversation with the lad from Bristol talking about agency driving and had kept it in the back of my mind for future reference......

ONWARDS AND (NOT NECESSARILY) UPWARDS

Once the dust settled, I phoned a number of agencies in Nottingham to see what sort of jobs they had to offer and whether they would take on someone with no experience. All that was needed to sign up was a driving licence and a visit to the office to answer some questions on the Highway Code. I think I signed up with 4 agencies at first and worried that I might be over stretching myself. What if they all phoned me up at once, offering work? What if I had to keep turning one or the other down due to already committing myself to working for another? No threat of that, only one called me the next day, the others never being heard from again.

I got a phone call on the Thursday asking if I could start on Monday at a well-known parcel delivery company. I nervously agreed and, after finalising directions to the place, I was told to be there for a 9.30am start. I liked the sound of the start time as I hadn't had to actually get up for work for 4 years.

The big day came and I arrived in the car park at 9.20.

I walked into the reception area and told them who I was, who had sent me, and why I was here. The lady directed me to wait with 6 other new start agency lads as someone would be along soon to instruct us. The warehouse worker arrived a few minutes later and paired each of us up with a regular driver so they could help us through and answer any questions we had.

The basic idea was that you were given a van and a route, and a massive pile of parcels. On each parcel was a route code. You could be given routes E4, G9, C17 and L6 so you would check through the cages and cages of parcels for everything with your route code on. This part of the process took the best part of an hour. Once all the agency lads got to know each other, we would all get together and sort the cages out, making piles of parcels for each of us which made the job a lot easier and quicker.

Once the massive pile of parcels was whittled down to slightly smaller piles for each load, we were given van keys and, having located your van in the yard and with it reversed onto the loading bay, loading would commence. On my first day I was given 48 drops which was, apparently, to start me off gently. I threw the parcels in the van and headed off with absolutely no idea which way round I would do my run. I had loaded the van quickly just to get me out of the depot quickly, figuring that it would be easier to sort the parcels out at each drop. How wrong could I have been? It was an absolute nightmare trying to find roads, the house names or numbers, and THEN having to try and find the corresponding parcels for the rest of the street in the back of the van. 3 times I went back to Alexandra Street in Kirkby-in-Ashfield as I hadn't realised I had more parcels for that street until I'd arrived at my next delivery 3 streets away. Lesson learned.

The next morning I was given 70 drops in the Lenton area of Nottingham. I sorted all my parcels in record time and reversed my van onto the bay. I then sorted all my parcels into roads, then bundled them together in areas. At the same time, I wrote each address on a piece of A4 paper along with the map page number and grid reference. I would then go through the map and sort out the best route as the last thing I wanted to be doing is double backing and crossing roads I'd already completed. The parcels could then be loaded into the van in drop order which made my life a lot easier.

Also, it is worth mentioning, this is in the days before Sat-Nav and we all relied on an A to Z style map book. Nowadays, the time could be used wisely punching postcodes into a Sat-Nav instead of writing down addresses and the corresponding page in a map book. How much easier must it be to just follow the arrow on a screen?

This job was the way it was to be for the next 2 months, the only grief coming from the locals. There was an occasion when I walked into a particularly rough block of flats in the centre of town clutching 8 bags of catalogue gear (obvious by the name splashed across the outside of the bags). After entry through a sliding security door I took the lift up to the 3rd floor surrounded by a group of scary looking lads eagerly eyeing up my wares. When the lift finally stopped at my floor, I rapidly embarked and headed for the first flat on the list. I knocked on the door, no reply. I knocked again, no reply. I turned around and knocked on the door of the flat opposite to see if they would be kind enough to take the parcel in for their neighbour. As my fist rapped the door, it creaked slowly open. I then noticed that the lock was broken and had been forced open. I also heard a shuffling noise coming from inside, so I decided to abandon the rest of the drops I had in the flats and, instead, take them back to the depot and claim no-one was in. It scared me, I can tell you, and I am not easily scared.

My run with this particular agency came to an end when another driver, who was employed through the same agency as I was working for, was arrested for trying to grab a 15 year old school girl and get her into his van. The girl, her parents, and the police all turned up at the depot and he was pointed out and taken away. As a result, all drivers from my agency were immediately told we wouldn't be needed anymore. A bit unfair on the rest of us, but understandable given the circumstance.

After this, I worked for a short time for a few different companies delivering anything from car windscreens to wooden gates, bread to alcohol and cigarettes. It was all mainly local work and quite boring. One job from around this time, working for a charity, stands out in my memory. This charity did (and still does) do great work in Eastern Europe, raising funds for, and building, shelters for young girls and ladies that have been rescued from the sex trade. There's no denying that the cause is honourable, but all the bosses were from the same family and it was very obvious, from the start, that they were lining their own pockets above everything else. My job was to drive a van, delivering items from their huge shop and collecting donated furniture etc. I usually had one or two helpers, but the work was still quite hard.

The obvious nature of the family's intentions became apparent when we collected a beautiful 3-piece suite from a house. The lady was happy to give it away, though she could have sold it for a lot of money, had she wanted to. It was in pristine condition and I have since seen the same style suite for sale, brand new, for over £3000. We arrived back at the shop and unloaded the suite carefully, the shop manager showing us where to place it. We all then stood round it, wondering how much it could be sold for. He reckoned £500, I said more, and he decided he would simply put a label on it reading 'offers' to see how much someone would be prepared to pay for it.

Whilst we were still pondering, the main boss appeared, having heard there was something rather special in the shop. She said how lovely she thought it was and how nice it would look in her living room. She then said that, as she had two dogs, they would ruin it, so it wasn't worth her buying it.

The next morning, on arriving at work, I enquired in the shop about the suite. It turned out that the boss had decided to buy it in the end, paying £200 for it. I was flabbergasted!! £200? It was worth hundreds more than that. It was unprofessional of her to buy it, especially for such a low price, as the charity could have made a lot more money from a member of the public buying it. This made me suspicious of the whole charity after that.

Not long afterwards, I was asked if I could do the 'clothing run'. I wasn't sure what this was, but agreed anyway. As was usual, I was given a couple of lads to help me out. The job was to empty the clothing recycling banks that you see dotted around the place, usually next to glass recycling facilities and also in the local refuse tip. What a horrible job that was. We were given large bags which we had to fill with the clothes and had to get stuck right in to them, up close and personal. My concern was that anything could be in amongst the clothes, drug needles for one, and I really didn't fancy getting Hepatitis or worse. Later that day, I developed an itchy, red rash up both arms, and refused to do this anymore. The young lads with me couldn't refuse, as they were taken on through some 'second chance' government initiative (which the charity got a lump sum payment for, in the region of £1000 per person I had heard).

The saddest part of this whole thing was the lies that the general public are told. The clothing banks are, to most peoples' knowledge, to recycle clothes so they will either be sent abroad or used in this country, to help the less fortunate, or sold in charity shops thus raising funds for those in need. There was very often baby clothes, lovingly washed and ironed, in excellent condition, put in to be recycled. So where does it all end up? It all gets dumped in a lorry trailer and taken to a huge factory where it is made into rags for industry. None of it is separated, none of it is sold as clothes, and it is all dumped in to together.

The only way I was going to get out of this was to start working my way up the road transport ladder.

GETTING BIGGER

Because I passed my car driving test before 1997, I was entitled to drive any vehicle up to 7.5 tonnes without taking another test. I feel sorry for young people these days as they have to pass a test to drive a car, then another test (costing around £1000) to drive a 7.5 tonne van before even contemplating driving a lorry. No wonder there's a shortage of HGV drivers, and it's getting worse. Anyway, I decided that driving something a bit bigger, for more money, was the best course of action. There would also be more opportunities for doing longer runs. I had considered this for a while so was well aware that I would have to know the ins and outs of driving a vehicle with a tacograph. This is to keep a record of how many hours you have driven, how many breaks you have had, how many kilometers the vehicle has driven (to stop fraudulent use) and whether the driver has had the correct amount of daily and weekly rest. I bought myself a couple of books to learn all about driver's hours and laws, and researched the subject thoroughly. I was aware, from reading the trucking magazines available, that there were heavy fines for exceeding the legal hours and fraudulent record keeping. The only thing I hadn't done was physically put a tacograph chart into a tacograph head on a vehicle. None of the books think to tell you which way round it goes. For the record (and assuming you haven't moved on to the much easier digital tacograph card) the wax side that the trace will appear on should be facing upwards when the tacho head is in the open position.

My first day was slightly marred by waking up late. I was supposed to arrive at the client for 05:30 but, for some reason, my alarm failed to ring, so I woke up at 05:30! The depot was the other side of town so I phoned them to tell them I'd be late, as well as a lot of apologising. I hate being late.

When I arrived, no-one said a word about the time so I assumed they weren't too bothered. My vehicle was already loaded for me with 2 drops; Hull and Grimsby. This is more like it, I thought. I took this opportunity to ask another driver to show me how to put the tacho chart in, which he kindly helped me with, and it was actually very simple. I climbed into the high Iveco cab (well, it felt high to me) and fired up the engine. I selected first gear and looked for the handbrake. My hand automatically went to look for a handbrake lever on the floor between the seats, where you'd normally find it in a car or van.

Nothing. Hmmm, a quick look round found an odd looking lever on the dashboard, which I moved to the up position and, with a hiss of air, I was on my way.

It was a pretty uneventful drive up the A1 and M18, I was just taking it all in and taking my time. I was pleased I only had 2 deliveries as I could take my time and get used to the vehicle and how it handled. I got my first delivery off in Hull with no problems and phoned in to let the controller know. I also asked how I would get over the Humber Bridge, and would they pay me back the money for the toll? Did they have a special account, or card I could use? I had no clue. The person on the phone said not to worry about it and just to go around the long way via the M62/M18/M180. Now, anyone with a small amount of geographical knowledge of the UK will know that the short bridge crossing saves just over an hour of driving (roughly 70 miles). I have never understood this. Apart from it being a complete and utter waste of fuel (and let's face it, most haulage firms plead poverty and moan about rising fuel costs), it's also dreadful for the environment. I was disappointed that people, in this day and age, weren't a little bit more aware of this.

Drop number 2 was delivered with no problems and I headed back to the depot, unloaded my empty cages out from the lorry, and parked up. I felt good as I had successfully completed my first day on a 'big' vehicle.

Incidentally, I was called in to this firm a couple of weeks later on a Saturday morning. My job for the day was, along with another agency driver, to take a van around 10 newsagents in Nottingham, Leicester and Lutterworth and swap boxes of chocolate bars. The reason for this was the chocolate company had started running a competition on the wrappers, so we had to take away the old bars and replace them with the new. The old bars were still in date by a long way and would probably be out of date by the time the competition was over, so in all probability, they would have been binned. Yet another waste of money and fuel. Two drivers in on a Saturday at time and a half, doing the job that one person could easily manage. We weren't complaining though!

I had been working for a week of holiday cover in Derbyshire, driving a Transit flatbed delivering wrought iron for an ornamental iron gate makers, when I received a phone call from the agency asking if I would be happy to work in Newark the following week? I was glad of the change as, though the driving part of this job wasn't too bad, there was a lot of time when I was standing around and they would find you work cleaning up the yard or sweeping out the warehouse. I have always thought that a driver should be just that. If you want a cleaner or yard man, hire one. The job had me delivering gates to customers or taking iron to a galvanizer near Sheffield, so it wasn't too taxing, but the delivery part of the job was just not busy enough for my liking.

On the Friday afternoon, I received another call from the agency saying that the job they had booked me for the following week had been cancelled, but they had something else for me, this time based in Derby, if I was interested? I wasn't in any position to turn work down, so agreed. I was given the address and the only details I got was 'paper collection'.

I arrived on the Monday morning at 7am, fresh from the weekend and willing to work. I was introduced to John, with whom I would be sharing driving duties with. Sharing? I never signed up for this! I'm a loner!! I was also told that we would be carrying out roadside collections around Derby of recycled paper. This was when home recycling was a reasonably new thing. In Derby, residents would leave a blue bag on the pavement outside their home which we would collect, empty into the cage on the back of our lorry, and leave an empty bag behind. It didn't sound too bad in principal.

We started off and I found early on that I needed to pretty much run everywhere, if we had any chance of getting the job done in a reasonable time. Couple this with the fact that this was the hottest day that Britain had seen for something like 5 years. Some of the bags were heavy (it's amazing how much paper people can cram in them) and they were often covered in dog piss where they had been left on the street. What a horrendous job that was. Actually, I was doing alright up to a point. I collected for half an hour, then swapped over with John so he would collect and I would drive. By 2pm, we had finished our round (in good time John admitted) so I thought that would be that. Apparently it normally would have been, just not today. Another driver was struggling due to the agency driver he had been assigned being slow and useless. John, for reasons only known to himself, agreed to help out with his run! I didn't get a say in the matter.

Off we went, by now soaked with sweat and very tired, to another residential estate where we started again. At one point, we stopped the lorry and jumped out, heading for a hose that a council gardener had left running, which we held in the air and stood under until we were soaked. It was that hot, we had to cool off somehow. I think it was eventually 6pm when we parked up back at the yard. The boss was waiting for us and did say that he appreciated what we had done. He said I was a good worker and would I be ok to come back tomorrow and, if so, he'd phone the agency and let them know? I politely declined. He then admitted that most agency workers walked off the job within a couple hours of starting so I did well to last the whole day.

On another occasion, I got asked by the agency to report to a local furniture delivery company as they required a driver for the week. I was told it would be 7.5 tonne work but it turned out to be, mainly, van work. It was an enjoyable job though, and pretty easy work, so I wasn't complaining. My first day saw me with drops in Leeds, Bradford, Halifax, Settle, Skipton and Ilkley. A lovely run out in some beautiful countryside and one of the few times when you do feel a bit of freedom on the road. Towards the end of the week, I was given a 7.5 tonne Iveco loaded with 2 drops in London, the first in Crouch End (not far from the Holloway Road) and the second in Woolwich. I love London, I have driven round all the sights extensively for pleasure (pleasure?) but, the idea of having to find somewhere to park to make deliveries did, and still does, fill me with dread.

Still, this day didn't look too hard and, with my trusty A to Z in my bag, I headed south on the M1 towards the 'Smoke'.

I arrived at the first drop, a furniture shop, at about 5.30am. I was told to be here for this time as there were parking restrictions all round and I would need to have my delivery done and be away before 6am. I bumped up on the pavement behind another van and waited. Another van pulled up behind me, also waiting to deliver to the same shop. The owner arrived at 20 minutes to 6 and immediately told me to get my wheels off the pavement as I would get fined if the traffic wardens saw it. I did this and opened the back ready to offload. Apparently, as always happens at this shop, the van in front needs to be offloaded first so that, when my furniture is unloaded, he will have room to load some of it straight onto him so he can get away. This was easy enough and I was leaving just as the Wardens were arriving at 5 minutes past 6.

I made my way onto the North Circular towards my next drop. I then took the Woolwich ferry across the Thames and found my second drop just round the corner, a small warehouse unit on an industrial estate. I parked outside and found the warehouse supervisor who instructed me to wait until bay 2 became available, it should be about half an hour.

Once the van had left bay 2, one of the warehouse lads signalled for me to reverse onto the dock. As I was reversing, an articulated lorry carrying a 40 foot container pulled up and started to reverse onto the empty bay next to me. I was, by now, inside the warehouse and opening the back of my lorry up ready to unload. This entailed me going into the back to pass out the flat-packs, the warehouse lads would take them off me, check them for damage, and carry them away. The artic driver came into the warehouse with his paperwork, opened the back doors of his container (which was full to the brim with boxes) and said "I'll be in my cab, give me a knock when you're done". Bloody hell, I thought, here's me sweating in the back unloading my lorry while he gets to sit in his cab and wait for someone else to do all the hard work. I found out from the guys in the warehouse that container drivers never, ever go into the container or help to unload as it's not their job. My day had gone smoothly but I couldn't help thinking back to that driver, sitting in his comfortable cab, whilst I was unloading cages of food and carrying them upstairs, or delivering steel that cut into your arms like a razor in various horrible jobs that I had after this.

When I arrived back at the yard later that day, I got loaded for the morning. The warehouse manager was impressed with the work I'd done that week and asked if I was looking for a job, as they may have an opening in a few weeks' time? Yes, I would like that! I took his phone number and said I'd call him.

I continued with this agency for a few weeks more but the money was not very good, so I decided to look around and see what was on offer. One particular agency I spoke to seemed promising. When I spoke to him on the phone he asked me "Has your wife got a photograph of you?" "Yes" I replied. "Good, she'll need it as she won't be seeing much of you!" I signed up a few hours later, filled in all the necessary forms and answered all the questions and was booked in for the following week.

I arrived at the client at 08:00 on the Monday, as my vehicle was just being loaded with the last few parcels. I always liked having the vehicle loaded as it meant I could get in and drive, instead of spending an hour or so in the depot. I didn't become a driver to be sociable, I enjoyed getting away, out on the open road. I later found out that the vehicle had been badly loaded, as it often was over the period I worked for this company, everything was dumped in as opposed to being in some sort of order. I took my paperwork and keys, and off I went. 42 drops in Leicestershire.

How the hell would I get them all delivered?

I didn't.

I think I managed 28 drops that first day. For a start, it took just over an hour to drive from the Nottingham depot to my first drop. Once I arrived, I couldn't open the rear shutter door. No one told me that the rear door had an annoying security lock that automatically locked every time the door was closed. The ignition key had a small square tag attached to it, which had to be 'swiped' over a sensor which was hidden somewhere under the back of the vehicle, at every drop, every time the back door needed to be opened.

The deliveries were to factory units, houses, farms, shops, you name it. All with the added complication of not being marked on the map, or not having a number or name visible from the road, or both. Also, you were never sure what you were actually delivering, it could be a pallet, a box, a jiffy bag, or any other odd shaped object that was rolling round in the back. The paperwork rarely gave you a clue as to what you were looking for and if it was loaded willy-nilly, it was like looking for a needle in a very large haystack.

When I arrived back at the depot that evening, they didn't seem to mind that I still had 14 drops undelivered. It was my first day so they gave me some leniency. I always hated taking drops back without good reason, it's a pride thing.

Day 2 came and off I go again, 45 drops today. Loaded again, I headed off down the M1 to get some of the distance out of the way before stopping just short of my first drop in a layby on the A5, just outside Lutterworth. I found all my drops on the map and, as with the first parcel delivery job I had done, wrote them all down with the map page and grid reference on a sheet of A4. This took about 45 minutes but was well worth it as I managed to get all 45 drops delivered. What a feeling as I drove north on the M1 at 3.30 that afternoon, empty, smiling away to myself, radio blaring, singing along.

I got back to the depot and, instead of being happy that I had completed my run, I got asked "Why didn't you answer your phone?"

"Huh?" I replied.

I bowed my head and rummaged in my backpack for my phone and there, on the screen, were 19 missed calls!

I hadn't heard it ring because of the radio and engine noise. Apparently, and they should probably have told me this before I left that morning, I should have phoned in once empty so I could start on my collections.

I had been working with this company for a few weeks doing the same run every day so knew my way around, not to mention where a lot of the drops were. This was fine, as it made life easier, I knew where I was going every day, and knew I would get all my deliveries and collections done. On this particular morning, I arrived at the office window to be told I was on the Derby run today. Damn! I'd have to learn a whole new area. Still, I set off with a positive attitude knowing that I'd managed to crack the Leicestershire route, so this shouldn't be too much of a problem, even if it takes me a day or so to get into the swing of it again.

Off I went, loaded as usual, into the bowels of Derby. I couldn't find the first few drops so pulled over and started looking at my map. Most of the postcodes were hard to fathom. Derby seems to have a strange postcode system, the numbers seemed to be all over the place. Anyway, I was in East Derby at around 11am when the cab phone rang. A lady was having her wardrobes fitted by a carpenter, the doors were in the back of my wagon, and the carpenter was waiting for them. She was all the way over to the west of town. Could I deliver them as soon as possible and how long would I be as they were getting desperate? I explained that I was all the way over the other side of the city, and it would take me ages to get to her, and back to where I was again. I agreed to take them over to her and spent over half hour retracing my route to get there (it doesn't sound like a lot but when you have this many drops on board, every minute counts). I eventually arrive and parked opposite the lady's house, in the only space available. I opened up the back door and tried to locate her wardrobe doors in the mountain of parcels. Clambering around like a monkey, I eventually found them right at the front, and over to the side. This particular lorry was a curtain-sider, which was utterly useless for this kind of job. Everything was piled high in the back, so you needed solid sides or else the load could shift and end up bulging the sides out. When I tried to pull the wardrobe doors out from the corner, they wouldn't move. They were firmly wedged between the curtain and the side of the lorry, also pinned in by all the other parcels and packages. I pulled and pulled, even the carpenter came out to help me and, between us both, we still couldn't shift them. I had to admit defeat so carried on from where I left off. I was now quite a way behind so knew I'd be taking undelivered parcels back to the depot. Oh well, not my fault this time. I eventually got enough of the load delivered to get to the doors, so I headed back to deliver them. Again, there was nowhere to park except opposite the lady's house, blocking someone's driveway. No sooner had I turned the ignition off, there was a knock on the door and an old man was ranting and raving that I couldn't park here as I was blocking his car from getting to the supermarket. I was always polite to people in this situation (unless they really pushed me) so explained that there was nowhere else to park and I'd be gone in 5 minutes. This wasn't good enough for him, he demanded I move NOW! I explained, still politely, that I'd be 5 minutes and suggested he let me get on with my delivery as it would only hold him up further if he kept me talking all day. That was it! He demanded to know my name and who I worked for. I did the same as I always do in this situation and said "The company name and number are on the cab door, my name is Gary, go and take it up with my firm as I'm done arguing with you." The carpenter came across and gave me a hand to carry the doors in, which took all of a couple of minutes (minus the lecture about where I should and shouldn't leave my lorry) and I was on my way. By now, I needed a tachograph break so headed down the road a short distance to have 30 minutes. The road was a cul-de-sac and, in all the time I was sat there, the old boy's car never moved. He can't have been that desperate to get to the shops after all. This is the kind of attitude that a driver will face on an almost daily basis. Everything is fine until you dare to block someone's driveway or car for a few minutes in the course of your work and they, all of a sudden, have an emergency for which they must simply get their car out NOW!

It was on this miserable day that I decided to give the furniture company a call as I had seen their advert in the local paper, looking for a driver. The thought of getting a job full-time at this company had been what kept me going over the last month or so of doing a ridiculous amount of multi-drop deliveries. I was even more miserable when I was told that, although they would love to have me work for them and had been very impressed with my work in the past, they would not be able to take me on as I had worked for them through an agency, and that agency would require the company to pay them if they were to employ me. This is the usual way when a company wants to employ an agency worker, the company can either keep paying the agency for a few months, or give them a lump sum payment. I was all for keeping it quiet and mentioning nothing to the agency but, unfortunately, they decided that it would be too risky.

I fortunately only worked for the multi-drop company for 6 weeks and, in that time, did get the offer of a full-time job (they must have been desperate, see last paragraph) which I politely declined. Still, it was regular, steady work, which I needed.

CAGED

During this period, I worked for a well-known major food delivery company, driving a Transit fridge van on local deliveries. I did really enjoy this as sometimes I would be sent 100 miles for 1 drop, maybe a pack of baked beans that was missing from their delivery. Again, not good for the environment (or the company accounts) but someone had to do it and I'm glad it was me. On other days, I might be sent out with 10 drops, but they were all fairly easy and there was no pressure to get the job done. The regular Transit driver was extremely lazy, I found out, and I was covering for him while he was off sick (which actually turned out to be 4 months). The transport manager and office staff were always really impressed with my workload as, apparently, the regular lad would load up in the morning with 4 or 5 drops, and not be seen again until the evening. I would be back again at lunchtime to load up for the afternoon. I wasn't showing off, or creeping, or even rushing, I just don't like taking advantage and would rather be working, than sitting in a layby doing nothing, as the day goes by much quicker.

It was coming to the end of summer, all the regular

drivers were back from their holidays, so this is usually a quiet time for agencies. One morning, the transport manager and operations manager approached me for a chat. They said the regular Transit driver would be back next week, so they can't offer me his job (though they did try to find a way of sacking him, but couldn't). Instead, they would like to take me on and pay for me to sit my Class 2 training. Class 2 would allow me to drive a rigid lorry up to 32 tonnes maximum gross weight. The training would cost around £1000 (assuming you passed first time and didn't need extra hours training and another test).

I said yes.

The following Monday I arrived at 06:00 as usual and was greeted with "What are you doing here? We haven't got any agency drivers in now as all our own drivers are back!" The agency hadn't bothered to tell me I was finished for the foreseeable future. I thought the company were supposed to be taking me on full-time? I was working there for 5 months and, after a while, the agency never phoned to ask if I was available or tell me what I was doing, so I just turned up for work every day. I assumed they'd tell me if I wasn't wanted though, surely? They may have been trying their luck though, which can happen. Some agencies will send an employee in to a company on the off-chance they can be used. It's very annoying for the employee as it's their time and fuel wasted.

When I got home, I spoke to the operations manager over the telephone to see if and when I was being taken on to start my training. He said they would have to reconsider the offer in a few months as they had all the drivers they needed at the moment, plus they were on a very strict budget so couldn't afford the extra training. All this after telling me 5 days before that they would put the ball in motion to get me taken on.

Things were getting desperate, none of the agencies had any work available. I scouted the paper for jobs. I have never claimed dole despite being out of work twice and wasn't about to start now. I would much rather dust myself off and get on with it. This may not always work but it has done me well so far.

I took a job with a nasty little father/son outfit located on an industrial estate just outside Nottingham. They had a fleet of older 7.5 tonne vehicles, plus some even older Transits. Every morning was the same; arrive for work and wait for your orders. Some of the runs were ok but other days, when work was quiet, they used to have you washing the whole fleet of vehicles. They didn't like to see people standing around (even if there was nothing to do) and, because of this, some people were known to have cleaned the whole fleet twice in the same day, just to keep busy and escape attention (and the boss's son). On one occasion they had me painting an old oil tank in the yard with bright orange paint. I refused to do it until they supplied me with overalls. They did so, but I knew I couldn't work there too much longer. What is it with these people that make them treat you like a kid? The boss owned a Bentley and, when things were quiet, he would have the drivers clean it. What an honour! The funny thing was, he would let us clean it with the same brushes that were used for the lorries and were usually left lying around on the ground getting covered with grit. I'll gladly clean your car! SCRAPE! SCRAPE!!

One day, they sent me off down to Brighton with 2 drops in an old 7.5 tonne lorry that would barely reach 50 mph and it started to concern me that I may not have enough driving hours* to get back to the yard the same day.

I headed slowly down to Brighton, delivered my 2 drops, and turned back towards Nottingham. When I got approximately an hour away from the yard, my 9 hours of driving were up. I am completely legal at this point as I had taken a 45 minute break after 4.5 hours of driving earlier in the day. I now needed to take another 45 minute break so I can drive for another hour and increase my driving hours to 10. I will just be able to make it back to the yard legally. The boss's son is waiting for me to get back so he can lock up the yard so I phone him to tell him I'm stopping for a break and will be back in roughly 1 hour and 45 minutes. He replied that I shouldn't need a break and to get back as soon as possible. I refused as I know I would be running illegally, something I have always refused to do. We have a short argument and he says he'll see me when I get back.

When I arrived back at the yard, he's jumping up and down and saying that it's only 4 hours down to Brighton, an 8 hour round trip. I explained that I had to run round between drops as no one was sure what to do with the delivery as it wasn't due until the following week and there was nowhere to store it. At one point, it looked like the whole load might be going back to Nottingham. I also explained that I got held up in slow moving traffic. He then said "You should have kept a record of your hours" to which I produced an A4 sheet with all my stop and start times, as well as breaks and unloading times, down to the nearest minute. This shut him up. It also reminded me to ALWAYS keep a record and NEVER trust anyone, even the company owner (who would get into trouble as well as the driver). It wasn't long after this when I treated myself to a Driver's Hours Guard, a compact device that recorded hours and breaks, so I could stop carrying around reams of paper for the same purpose.

My total hours of driving for that day were 9 hours and 56 minutes. I didn't work there any more after that.

Still, the few weeks I did work there kept me out of poverty so I was grateful. I also gained some good experience whilst working there, too. Thankfully, a couple of days before the Brighton run, I had received a call from my regular agency saying that I could start back at the food delivery job the following week. I was glad of this as the hours were good and the work was easy enough. I also knew that I would be there steady until Christmas, which was important.

I settled back into the routine very quickly and, before too long, I was again approached to see if I wanted to train for my Class 2 licence. This time I refused. It was a hard decision, but they had let me down last time, what was to stop them doing the same again?

As luck would have it, the agency I was working for had started to train drivers for their class 2 test. They had their own instructor and vehicle. The deal was that they would cover the full cost of training and test, and would take half of it back from the employee over a 3 month period. It sounded pretty fair and, before long, I had dreams of driving a huge truck all over the country. But first, the reality.....

*I will take the opportunity to explain driver's hours in simple terms (any drivers may want to skip this bit);

-The maximum driving hours in any one shift is 9 hours, but this can be increased to 10 hours on 2 days in any one week.

-After 4.5 hours of driving you must have a 45 minute break. This can be split into 2 breaks, but the second break must be a minimum of 30 minutes.

-Your working time in any one day must not exceed 15 hours and this includes driving time, breaks, other work i.e. loading, fuelling etc.

-A daily rest of 11 hours between shifts must be taken, but this can be reduced to 9 hours on 3 occasions in any 1 week.

There are other rules such as weekly breaks, the 6 hour maximum working time without a break to keep in line with the Working Time Directive and Period of Availability (POA). This is not a definitive guide, and is too complicated to simplify here, so I suggest you look up some of the good books available that will explain everything you need.

GOING UP!

I had been along and met my instructor at the agency office a few weeks previous, and had been taken out for a short assessment run, so wasn't nervous on my first day of training. The course was to be for 5 days, with the test held on day 5, a Friday. I was taking lessons with another lad, Steve, who I got on very well with. I always felt I'd be better with one-to-one tuition, but it worked out well as seeing someone else make mistakes meant you tried not to make the same mistakes yourself.

We met each day at the agency office and walked over to where the lorry was parked. It was an old Mercedes with a flat bed, which made reversing and all-round vision easier.

I was chosen to drive first as I had more experience driving 7.5 tonne vehicles than Steve had. We started the engine and set off on our way, immediately getting caught in traffic. We were booked in for our theory tests in an hour's time so really needed to get to Stoke-on-Trent as soon as we could. We made it in time and pulled up at the door and jumped out, our instructor taking the vehicle down to the road and waiting there with it. Sitting in the waiting room, both Steve and I were very nervous. There was really no need to be as the test was very easy. Steve got 33 and I got 34 out of 35.

Toucan crossing? What the hell is one of those? For the rest of the day we took it in turns driving around the city streets of Stoke and the country roads surrounding it. After lunch, we headed back to the yard where the lorry was kept and were shown the reversing exercise.

There are basically two coned boxes. You reverse out of one box and into the other, all the while missing the cones at the side and steering towards the next box, which is behind and to your left.

You should now be reversing in a straight line, diagonally between the two boxes.

Next, it is just a matter of bringing the rear of the vehicle into box 2 and stopping the rear overhang within a one metre box. Reverse too far and it's a fail. Hit a cone and it's a fail.

This is hopefully explained better in the diagram below;

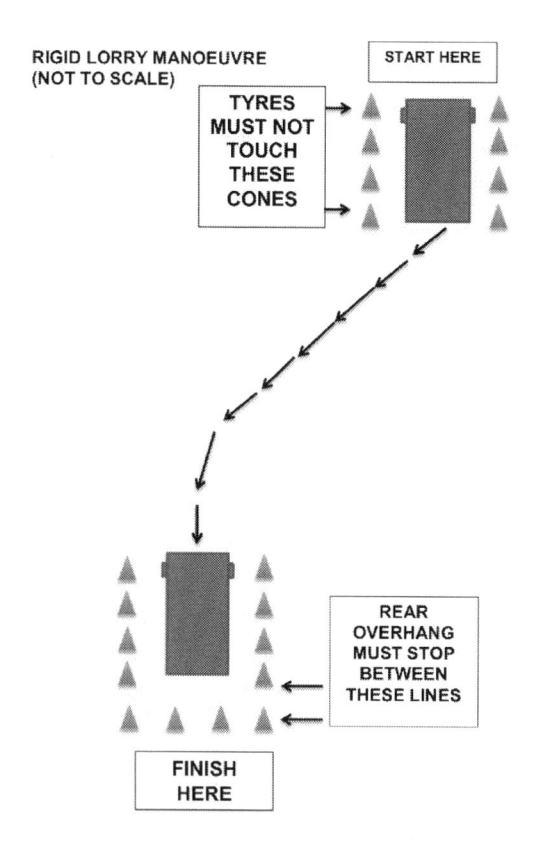

```
RIGID LORRY MANOEUVRE          START HERE
(NOT TO SCALE)
              TYRES      ▲        ▲
              MUST NOT            ▮
              TOUCH      ▲        ▮ ▲
              THESE      ▲        ▮
              CONES               ▮ ▲
                         ▲        ▮
                                  ↙
                                 ↙
                                ↙
                               ↙
                              ↙
                             ↓

              ▲        ▲
              ▲   ▮    ▲       REAR
              ▲   ▮    ▲       OVERHANG
              ▲   ▮    ▲   ←   MUST STOP
              ▲   ▮    ▲       BETWEEN
              ▲        ▲       THESE LINES
              ▲   ▲ ▲  ▲   ←

                  FINISH
                  HERE
```

Once we'd mastered the reversing technique, and emergency stop, the days relaxed into a routine. I would drive, then Steve would take over. After lunch we'd maybe practice the hill start and emergency stop, then back to some general driving and finishing the day with the reversing exercise back at the yard. It was actually a very enjoyable week. Our instructor was friendly, enjoyed a good laugh, and was always regaling us with anecdotes and tales of the road. We also picked up a lot of useful information from him, especially about driving articulated lorries.

Thursday came and went far too quickly, and Friday was test day. We set off in the morning for some general driving round town followed by some last minute braking exercises. We were both obviously very nervous and I gave one of the worst drives imaginable. I managed to clip 2 kerbs (a big no no!) and was generally unhappy with my performance. Steve managed to break the nearside door mirror off by getting too close to an overhanging branch.

It all seemed very ominous.

I chose to be tested first, mainly because I couldn't stand sitting around nervous for another hour while Steve took his test, I would rather get it over and done with. Steve was more than happy for me to go first.

First up was the reversing exercise, which seemed to go ok. Our vehicle was fitted with a large round nut on the rear driver's side mudguard and stuck out just far enough so you could see it in the mirror. When this lined up with the front line of the box, the rear overhang would be pretty much central in the one metre box. It worked every time. I believe most instructors have a method for this which usually involves a nut or paint.

By now, it was pouring with rain and next was the emergency stop (well, it's actually called a 'controlled stop'). The vehicle has to be stopped quickly, in a safe manner, with minimal loss of grip, and in a short distance. Air brakes don't make this easy and they can be hard to get used to. Touch them gently and they will not seem to be doing anything at all, let alone slowing you down. Press them a bit harder and you, along with all your night-out gear that was carelessly left on the bunk, will be through the windscreen.

I was instructed to pull up to the first line. From there, I was told to accelerate to 10mph and, at the second line on the road, brake. This all went well despite the rain. The rest of the test is a bit of a blur, I was just going through the motions and trying not to think too much about the situation. I was convinced I'd failed on a couple of occasions. The first was in a little village, only a few miles from the test centre. I could see a mini roundabout ahead but, between me and it, and for quite some distance, was a line of parked cars on both sides of the road leaving just enough room for one way traffic. Cars whizzed from the right of the roundabout, heading straight for me. If I moved, I would be impeding their progress. FAIL! If I waited here for too long, it could be construed that I'm hesitant. FAIL! In the end, I saw a gap, and went for it. The next incident happened just after this. I had driven through a village with a 30mph speed limit and, thinking I knew this road quite well as we had travelled along it on numerous occasions over the last week, assumed I was in the 40mph limit which followed. I wasn't. Luckily for me, the road climbed quite a steep hill. I had my foot to the floor trying to accelerate to 40, but was being held back to 30 by the slope. I could see my examiner looking at my feet twice. I assumed he was looking to see that I was aware I was in a 40 limit. He wasn't, he was probably looking and wondering why I was trying to accelerate above 30 in a 30 limit. I looked up and saw the 40 signs and panicked, but was extremely lucky that I was unable to accelerate due to the hill. I then assumed I'd failed and relaxed into the rest of the test thinking I had nothing else to lose and may as well enjoy the ride and prepare for test number 2. I was astounded when we arrived back at the test centre to be told that I had passed with 8 minor faults. He did mention hesitating in the village and I explained that it wasn't an easy choice, to which he agreed. He thankfully didn't mention the other incident!

During the hour that Steve was taking his test, I did get the chance to watch a lad unhitching his trailer as part of his Class 1 test and, yet again, decided it looked pretty hard and that I would probably never get round to having a go myself. It didn't help that it was still pouring with rain. I then went for some food with my instructor (I hadn't eaten all day due to nerves) and waited for Steve to finish his test. Unfortunately, he wasn't so lucky. He clipped a kerb and didn't do too well on his hill start. I felt sorry for him as it would have been good to have both passed together. I was glad to hear that he went back a week later and passed.

I passed my test on the Friday and was back in at the food supplier on the Monday. This time, I was driving a proper lorry. They had a fleet of Scania trucks, some old, some new. I couldn't wait to get on the road so I was paired with a driver's mate and off we went.

Most of the drops were easy enough, but some were very tight to get into. One school had a very tight access road that I had to reverse into so the mate jumped out to help guide me in. I managed it with no problems and he told me that the week before, he'd been out with one of the experienced drivers, and the guy struggled to get in here, taking 3 attempts. There's no shame in this, but it did boost my confidence. Once parked, we had to struggle getting cages off the lorry and carry everything upstairs to the kitchen, as was often the case. It was good experience, though.

After a few weeks on this job, I was getting itchy feet. I longed for a motorway journey to somewhere new. I told the agency that I needed a change and they kindly managed to get me a week on general haulage.

Wow! This is a bit more like it. Proper trucking!

My first day was very easy. My curtain-sided lorry was to be loaded for one drop in Micheldever Station, just off the A34, not far from Winchester. I arrived to pick up my truck at 7am as instructed, only to be told it was parked in a yard 6 miles away. I took the keys and headed for the other yard. The lorry was an old Iveco and had, sadly, seen better days. I got my night out gear stowed away and tried to clean the cab out as best as I could. I washed the windscreen but the wipers wouldn't stop. They carried on for about 20 minutes down the road, I even turned the ignition off but they still didn't stop. What a great start to the week this was!

The rest of the day went without a hitch and I was told to start at 7am again the following morning. On arriving at the yard, my lorry was being loaded with 6 pallets, 2 for Blackpool and 4 for Leyland. This seemed like it could be another easy day so I set off on my journey with a smile on my face. I got both drops delivered in good time and was then instructed to head to Oldham, where I would be loading a train bogey for Stratford, East London. The train depot was easy to find (just follow the railway) and they loaded me as soon as I arrived. I headed across the M62 and south on the M6, heading for London. Halfway across the Thelwall Viaduct the phone rang. Would I be able to load another bogey tonight in Derby, also heading for Stratford? I cut across the

A50 towards Derby and managed to find a take away en route, as my lunchtime sandwiches were long gone and it was now evening. After enjoying my meal, I headed to the second collection point and, by the time I had loaded up, my 15 hour daily limit was reached. The kind security guard said it was ok to park just outside the gate and he'd be on all night so would keep an eye on me.

My first ever night out in a truck.

I awoke the next morning and had a quick breakfast of Weetabix and a cup of tea. I switched the night heater on as it had turned chilly, it would also clear the condensation from the windows. I got dressed and jumped out of my truck, shutting the door behind me to keep the heat in. I washed my breakfast bowl and mug, relieved myself and headed back to the cab. My door wouldn't open. The driver side door had somehow locked itself. Obviously it was unlocked when I jumped out, I hadn't locked it behind me, so what the hell was wrong with it?? I knew the passenger door was still locked, but tried it anyway in the false hope that it had somehow unlocked itself. Back round the driver's side, I could see the ignition keys dangling from the ignition. Shit! shit! SHIT!! Most of the time, if you do something wrong, or stupid, or embarrassing, there's often a way that it can be hidden, or covered up. I'm pretty sure most of us look for the easy option in such circumstances. It's not a case of being dishonest, it's more a case of not wanting to look a complete and utter prat. There was no way out of this though. My gear was inside the cab, as were the keys. I was outside the truck. I couldn't even get a taxi home and hide under the kitchen table waiting for the all clear, as all my gear and maps were still imprisoned within. Not that I would have done, you understand, but these things flash through your mind in that split second before rational thinking reappears. It could have been a lot worse: I may have dived out for a piss in the middle of the night without getting dressed and be stuck in a much worse predicament.

Still, how the hell was I going to get out of this without anyone finding out? I know! I'll try the door handles again! Nothing. Obviously. In fact, I tried so hard that the plastic passenger handle came off in my hand, completely snapped. I then had another brainwave....if I could open the outside locker on the passenger side, I may just be able to reach in through a gap and undo the door lock! The side locker opened from the outside, so that bit was easy. I reached in as far as I could, standing on tiptoe, but just couldn't reach the handle. I was so close, I could feel the plastic surround and I even tried hooking it with a bit of wire, but to no avail. I knew there was only one thing for it.

I entered the security hut and explained my dilemma to the guard. He let me use his phone to call up my company as my phone, of course, was locked in the cab. About an hour later, one of the other drivers came out with a spare set of keys. I felt a total idiot but at least it was now over and I could get on my way. Incidentally, the security guard said he used to be a driver and always kept his lorry keys in his pocket, even if only jumping out for a second. This advice has stuck with me and I still keep my keys in my pocket every time I leave the cab, 15 years on.

Despite this setback, the rest of the week went very well and I had collections and deliveries in Leicester, St Albans, Luton, London, Birmingham and Scunthorpe. I felt like I was truly becoming a trucker, except for the moment I nearly wrote off a car behind me at some traffic lights in Tipton, just outside Dudley. I had collected a load of second/faulty vacuum cleaners from a warehouse in Luton for delivery in Tipton. A guy buys them by the pallet-load and fixes them up to sell them on. I was doing well for time having spent the night at Frankley services on the M6 as I wanted to get in early when the guy opened so I could be on my way again and not hit too much traffic. I pulled up at a set of traffic lights on a hill, applied the handbrake, and waited. When the lights for the other road changed, I selected first gear and was ready for pulling away. As soon as the light changed to green, I released the brake, lifted the clutch and gave the engine good revs to get up the slope. This is all textbook stuff, except the fact that I was actually in reverse gear rather than first. Reverse gear is next to first on the vehicle and slipped in very easily.   The lorry shot back about 3 metres.   I managed to slam on the brakes and, luckily, the car behind had left a huge gap so there was no risk of a collision.   It shook me up though and I went back to pulling away in second gear as there would be no confusion in future.

When I got back to the yard on the Friday the boss asked me if I was looking for a job as he would have a position available in a couple of weeks, so I can't have been a bad driver for the week.   Either that or he was desperate!   He did ask about the door handle and I denied it saying that it was like that when I picked the vehicle up.   He said he knew it wasn't but didn't push the issue.   Don't ask me why I did that, probably because I felt embarrassed enough about getting locked out of the cab.

LET'S ROCK 'N' ROLL

I was now 'between jobs' again. The agency work had gone quiet and there were no real jobs in the paper, which I scoured regularly. One advert did catch my eye, though. It was a part time driving job, Class 2 licence required, to drive a tour bus for a well-known Meat Loaf tribute act. This looked like it could suit me well, being into music and the whole rock 'n' roll lifestyle. I phoned the number and the guy explained he was desperate for a driver, having been let down for a gig they had coming up on the Saturday night in Skegness. This sounded good to me so I arranged to meet him that afternoon where the bus was parked.

I drove into the yard, where I met Steve, and there it was, a huge, proper sized, tour bus. This could be fine. He showed me round, it had a seating area at the front, 8 bunks in the mid-section, and a kitchen/dining area at the rear. There was no downstairs as such but, if you climbed down the stairs at the rear, there was a toilet which wasn't actually plumbed in so out of use. Underneath the bus were 4 huge pods, full of lighting rigs, instruments, and a PA system. He explained that he only gigged a couple of nights a week and sometimes, on the rare occasion, they would play 3 concerts over a weekend. I would get £80 a gig, regardless of how many hours I worked.   It seemed quite fair.

The bus was being fixed that afternoon so I didn't get a test drive but I agreed to drive the band to Skegness on the Saturday and he thought it best if I came down early for a quick run as the gearbox was a bit 'quirky'.

Saturday came and I arrived about an hour before everyone else. Steve was there to meet me and we set off for a quick run round the block. The gearbox was a bit difficult to use, but nothing I wouldn't get used to. I was pretty nervous as I wasn't used to driving people around but they seemed like a nice enough bunch. One of them explained that the last driver had actually been sacked as his driving was atrocious. They would be in their bunks, trying to sleep on the journey home, and he would be driving down the motorway and rocking them all over the place. On the last occasion he drove the bus, they were all sat round the dining table, hanging on for grim death! All small movements are magnified at the top of a bus, so the driver needs to be as smooth as possible.

With everyone boarded, we set off along the A17 for Skeggy heading for a real class venue; Butlins! I managed to drive the bus nice and smoothly and heard no complaints from the passengers. Most of them had a chat and were keen to find out more about my drumming.

We arrived at the venue and found somewhere to

park near the doors, to ease the unloading process. My job was to drive (obviously) and to connect up the coach's power line. After that, I was free to do what I wanted. I'd generally help with the load-in, and set up the merchandise stall, which I would man during the interval. At one time or another, I would be asked to head into town and hunt down some batteries or guitar leads. There were 5 musicians, a drummer, guitarist, bass player, keyboard player, and backing singer, plus Steve, and as well as the driver, we carried a soundman and lighting engineer, who all doubled as roadies. It was quite interesting, from my point of view, to learn a bit more about the stage set up and gear that a touring band needs on the road. This first night, choosing not to get in the way, I was content to sit back and watch how everything worked.

The gig came and went and we set off back towards Nottingham. The night was icy cold and the road was sparkling with ice. It was pretty scary to think of all those peoples' lives in my hands.

I held this job for a couple of months and, for the most part, enjoyed it. Some of the gigs were good, in beautiful old theatres such as the White Rock Theatre in Hastings. Other gigs were not so good, the Tipton Working Men's Club springs to mind! Still, it was all an experience and my job was easy enough.

One weekend we headed south to play Bournemouth and Torquay. I got harassed in Bournemouth by an old woman. She was a massive Meat Loaf fan and was desperate to meet Steve, or 'Meat' as she called him. Every time I left the bus to go into the venue, she would be waiting to pounce on me, demanding to be let into the bus. Steve didn't want to come out, I wasn't about to let her in, so just had to put up with her. She said that 'Bat Out Of Hell' was her favourite song ever, and she couldn't wait to see it performed that night. Funnily enough, she left the concert early and was hassling me on the merchandise stand whilst the song was playing. She said she was disappointed that he hadn't played it, and was a bit dismayed when I told her it was playing right now and she was missing it. Pretty sad, but I think you'd have to be to follow a Meat Loaf tribute act about.

There was a Meat Loaf look-a-like, also living in Bournemouth. He had a better personalised car number plate than Steve had. Steve was jealous of this fact, plus the fact he had to wear a wig as he was bald as a coot. The look-a-like, despite having lovely flowing hair, was, apparently, jealous of Steve as, although he looked the part, he couldn't sing a note. I found this whole scenario hilarious and vowed never, ever to play in a tribute band, no matter how desperate I was for money or 'glory'! (Not that I ever would have done anyway).

Steve was a bit of an egotist, and was always shouting at the other band members. I remember one occasion when the band had set up ready for a sound check and Steve was still on the bus. The drummer was trying to nail a rhythm that he had picked up somewhere. The lighting bloke, Dave, also played drums and, between them, they were seeing if they could play it. I went on to the bus for a cup of tea and Steve immediately barked "Tell them two idiots to shut up that racket". I went in and told them that Hitler had spoken and they sulked off quietly to their various corners.

Steve had also taken to telling me how to drive. He had the most irritating Lancashire accent, sort of like a whiny Fred Dibna, if you can imagine that? One morning, we were driving down the A42, eventually heading for that night's gig in Reading. It was winter and there was snow on the dual carriageway. The slow lane was clear, and everyone was behind one another, taking it steady. Lane 2 was full of snow, and not many drivers were braving overtaking for fear of sliding. Steve decided we should be going a lot faster and barked "Gary, are you going to overtake or are we going to sit here all day, we'll be late, we need to be there by 4!" I ignored him and could hear him moaning. I then bawled back at him "I am not risking sliding or having an accident so, if you want to go faster, you drive the f*cking thing!" This quietened him down. On another occasion, we had only just left Nottingham when he started up. "Go a bit faster, go a bit faster". So I did. The next set of lights changed to red as I was nearly upon them, so I slammed on the brakes. Much whining ensued "Gary, Gary! Don't brake so hard!!" I lost the plot at this point and told him that if he didn't stop moaning, I would turn round and take the bus back to Nottingham, leaving him to sort someone else out to drive. He then protested saying that I shouldn't have stopped at the red light, I should have driven through! It's my licence, I'm not risking it for him or anyone else!!!

Karma caught up with him though on a couple of occasions. One time, he had told me to keep an eye on the smoke coming from the exhaust as it was starting to look worse. We were on the M40 and I kept checking the mirrors but could see no smoke. All of a sudden, a police car pulled up alongside me and indicated for me to leave the motorway at the next exit. Once safely parked, the policeman explained that there is too much smoke coming from the exhaust and we'd have to fix it before continuing our journey. We were lucky they didn't take any further action (or, seeing as I was the driver, I was lucky). We found an industrial estate to park in and sort the problem out. He moaned that I should have kept a watch for smoke, which I had, but why wasn't he watching through the back window as well? The problem was easily sorted so should not even have been an issue as it could have been fixed before we left.

Another time, we left Torquay at midnight, which

would get us home early the following morning. As I was going to have to drive through the night, I said I would try and get some sleep instead of selling merchandise. This made him moan "Who's going to sell it, then?" Not my problem. Luckily for him, the soundman said he would rush out in the interval, and at the end of the night, to keep an eye on things. I set the stall up, closed the shutter, and headed off to my bunk on the bus.

We left Torquay and I said the fuel looked low. Steve would only allow me to fill up with £70 at a time, despite the bus having huge tanks. I wasn't sure what the reason for this was but he claimed the credit card company would only allow £70 at a time (a bit odd seeing as we always paid with cash). I suspect it was so he didn't have an £800 bill for fuel before he had made the money back from the gig. I pulled into a petrol station a few miles up the road and, as was usual, everyone left the bus to get themselves some food or a coffee. I put £70 worth of diesel in the tank, paid, and after making sure everyone was back on the bus, turned the key. Nothing. I tried again. Nothing. The engine was turning over but not firing. This caused him to moan further about the fact we hadn't needed fuel (we did, I knew by now how much fuel there was in the tank and how far it would get us). The pods had to be emptied to access the engine and, seeing as most people had retired to their bunks for the journey, it was up to Steve to roll up his sleeves to get the problem sorted. To give him his due, he did get the engine going again, but it took an hour or so.

I was about finished with this job so, once we were back home after that night, I told him I wouldn't be driving for him anymore. I don't mind doing my job, even getting a bit of grief, but this was getting ridiculous. It wasn't just the journey, we all had to share the bus for the weekend, sleeping on top of each other (literally, the bunks were the size of a coffin), hanging around and eating together. He was starting to irritate me too much to have to spend time with him.

CAGED (AGAIN)

The following week I was back to reality with a bump, delivering cages of food for the same company again.

I was starting to hate this job.

My first drop on the Monday was to a large hotel in Nottingham. I was alone on this particular day and was stacking the frozen food up when the head chef came whizzing down the corridor, riding a drinks trolley. He crashed straight into the boxes I had neatly stacked, saying nothing. I angrily started to stack the boxes back up.

He said "You don't throw those boxes like that"

I said "Excuse me?"

He repeated himself.

I told him that he'd just knocked them over and I am restacking them.

His reply? "No I didn't!"

An argument ensued which ended with me signing the paperwork myself and throwing it in the air before storming out.

It is not good to have your blood boiling before 7am.

Things like this happened regularly in this job, unfortunately. On numerous occasions I would be sent on a run that I didn't know, maybe 30 drops across 3 counties. If the regular driver was away, he may not have told the warehouse lads the order that the lorry should be loaded. At every drop I would have to dig around in the back, trying to push cages out of the way to extract one that could be buried 3 cages deep. Not easy in a confined space, even harder when dealing with a steep camber of the road, not to mention high blood pressure.

A DAY IN THE LIFE

One extremely damp morning in deepest rural Leicestershire, I had been sent out with 30 drops starting with a delivery to a holiday camp. At most drops like this, time was wasted trying to find the kitchens. This place was no exception, but after a while I saw the familiar sight of the chimney and dustbins which usually belonged to the kitchen. I started unloading the 6 cages for this drop and wheeled them into the kitchen. The contents were then unloaded onto a long, stainless steel, work surface, with the usual "Frozen here" and "Tins there" from the chef who watched me all the while I was unloading. 20 minutes later the cages were empty and I handed him the paperwork to sign. He said "Just wait a minute while I check everything" and proceeded to poke about the order. I protested, explaining that he'd been stood watching me for 20 minutes and should have checked it then. He told me I had no choice but to wait. We'll see about that! I told him that I was going to take the empty cages back to the lorry and if he hadn't finished by the time I got back, I would sign the paperwork myself. Luckily, he was just finishing up when I came back in and handed me the signed piece of paper. I know it sounds like I'm being awkward, but when you consider that I may have to go through this with 20 or 30 people in a day, every day, it becomes very tedious. Also, those wasted 10 minutes on every drop add up to a lot of time sat waiting for someone to do something they should have done while I was unloading. Every second counts when you are new to a run and have to find all the drops for the first time.

A few more drops delivered, then next on the list was Oakham Prison. I hated delivering to prisons as it was always tedious getting in and out, plus I always got the unsettling feeling that they wouldn't actually let me out. The usual procedure was to queue up outside (luckily I was first in line) and wait for the gates to open. Once in to the space known as the 'airlock', the gates behind would be locked and my vehicle, load, cab, and sometimes belongings, would be searched. Mobile phones are taken from you too. The second gate would now be opened and I could drive through. Generally, a guard would walk in front of you and guide you to the kitchens, or canteen, so you never got lost.

On this occasion, I had a load of chocolate and drinks for the canteen. Unfortunately, this was the visitors' canteen as opposed to the guards' canteen, or even the prisoners' canteen. This particular canteen was much like the canteens I had visited in other prisons, full of women and screaming babies, all waiting to visit their beloved boyfriends and husbands, who were probably inside for assault or murder. A lovely bunch, to say the least. I wheeled the cage in and this ugly, fat, fag-stinking women waddles over and says "'ere, look at this twat, who does he think he is, delivering at this time, why didn't he come earlier?" The rest started to mumble too, but I couldn't catch what they were saying but I think the general gist of it was that I shouldn't be in the way when they need to buy chocolate for whomever they were visiting (or to shut their kids up). I ignored them all and the guard looked at me as if to say "Ignore them" The guard entered the store room and I wheeled the cage in, but it would only go in so far, and he was now trapped in the store, with me outside. All I could do was watch him unload the boxes and stack them on the shelves, I couldn't get round to help. I apologised and told him that was my job but he said he didn't mind. Then from behind me, Miss UK pipes up again "'ere, look at 'im now, leaving that poor old man to do all the work, he should be ashamed of 'imself!" I ignored her again but the irony was not lost on me. Minutes before, she would have hated the 'screw' just for his job, making life a misery for her partner. Also, I don't suppose she or her partner, or her kids, have or will ever see a day's work in their lives. Not an honest days' work, anyway. I was glad when the cage was empty and I was well away from that place.

My next delivery was a garden centre. I pulled into the car park, near to the main entrance. A man came running over, shouting that they had just had a very expensive new tarmac car park laid (it did look nice) and I shouldn't be parking on it. No one told me, and it was too late now. This, again, set me up in a good mood, especially as I had to wheel 4 heavy cages all the way through the centre to the kitchens, dodging customers and expensive garden ornaments.

The office phoned and said they were sending another driver out to take a few drops from me as I wasn't managing too well. I got to the meeting point and had to wait another 45 minutes for him to arrive. It was nice to have a break, and was grateful that he lightened my load (he did take the easy drops, I noticed) but I was now well behind schedule, even with less drops to do.

My last drop on this particular day was in Melton Mowbray. By now, it was pouring with rain. I reversed round towards the kitchens but couldn't get very close so had to roll the cages over rough ground to get to the door. I unloaded the cages, mainly full of boxes of chilled and frozen food, and took it down to the kitchen door. It was locked. Damn!! I banged and banged. I was now soaked, as were the boxes. As I rolled them back up towards the lorry, one of the wheels caught in a rut and the cage tipped towards me. The door wasn't secured closed properly (most of the cages were knackered and didn't shut) and, even though I managed to stop the cage from fully tipping over, most of the boxes fell out onto the ground. I picked them up, threw them back into the cage, and stamped on them with my size 12 boots for good measure. I had, by now, well and truly lost the plot, and was so angry that I didn't care. On arrival back at the depot, I had to explain how the boxes came to be in such a state. The top boss was called down and actually believed my story of how they came to be crushed. Not one of my best decisions, but stress can do that to a person, especially after a day like I'd just had.

ON AND ON IT GOES...

A few weeks later I was delivering around Sheffield. I knew this route as I had been shown the week previously by the regular driver, Simon. I was going great. I was on drop number 5, a bingo hall, on the outskirts of town. Open the door, dump the load just behind, job done. "At this drop" Simon had told me, "Sort out the cages for the next delivery, an old people's home." I decided that, as I was getting on so well, I would forgo this and, instead, sort out the cages at the next drop. Now, the vehicle I had for this run was a brand new Scania. The company, in their infinite wisdom, had decided to come up with an easier, better way of securing the cages in the back.

The older vehicles had a freezer compartment at the very front of the van, just behind the cab, and this could be accessed through a door in the side of the vehicle. Behind this was a moveable bulkhead to separate the freezer from the chiller behind and each area could have its temperature controlled independently. The cages were secured with a ratchet strap width ways across the vehicle.

The new vehicles had a freezer compartment that ran front to rear of the vehicle, one cage in width and again with a moveable partition. Looking in from the rear of the vehicle, the freezer would be to the left (1 cage wide) and the chiller to the right of this (2 cages wide). The new arrangement meant that the cages were now secured with a bar from floor to ceiling and securing into rails. This created problems if you needed the three rear cages for a drop as you had to remove three of the securing bars, whereas with the older model only one strap would have to be removed. Also, the space in the back is very limited if the lorry was fully loaded so there is no room to juggle cages about.

Anyway, onwards I plough towards the old people's home. I have been here before so know exactly how to find it, and the kitchen. I reverse down the slope (I'm sure you can see what's about to happen, pity I didn't stop to think things through) and drop the tail lift, raise it to the 'up' position, still marvelling at how well I'm doing for time. I check the cages I need, 1 frozen and 2 chilled. I open the freezer door and remove the securing bar. BIG MISTAKE!! The frozen cage starts rolling towards me, pushed by the weight of 8 other frozen cages following along behind it! I try to hold it back but have absolutely no chance so take the only other option I have at this point; I leap from the tail lift, which is about 5 foot off the ground, and roll out of the way. As I lay there on the ground, I looked up to see the rear cage hit the raised flap on the tail lift and tilt dramatically towards me. It seemed to pause there for a few seconds, as if it was deciding whether to settle back down or jump off and flatten me and then, luckily for me, it settled back to the normal position and everything went quiet. My pulse was racing. I stood up and dusted myself down checking for any extra holes, lumps or misshapen bits on my body. None, phew! Some drivers don't bother to raise these flaps, I'm not sure why. They've obviously never been in the situation I'd just been in, or think they could ever be in that position. Had the flaps been down, all 9 cages would have ended up in a buckled heap on the ground with thousands of pounds worth of damaged food. I would have had a lot of mess to clean up and a lot more explaining to do. That's if I had moved out of the way quickly and not have been crushed underneath.

I learned my lesson months before when delivering to a shop in the centre of Rugby and, having parked on a very slight camber (not even noticeable unless you carry around a pocket-sized spirit level), I proceeded to move the cages onto the tail lift. As I turned away I noticed one very heavy cage full of cans of drink, rolling slowly towards the pavement side of the tail lift. I reached out and grabbed it and managed to wrestle it into a safe position. There were no side flaps on that particular lorry and, for a few moments, the cage teetered above pedestrians (including children) walking oblivious underneath. I shudder to think what could have happened if it had fallen.

Some lifts only have short flaps which just serve to 'trip up' the cage, sending it toppling over and ending up on the ground in a mass of broken eggs, a cloud of flour and leaving only a trail of cream trickling down the drain.

Chilling.

By that description, you have probably guess that yes, again, this has happened to me. It's not that I'm stupid (I don't think) or careless, things just sometimes work out this way. I was delivering a Christmas order for (yet again) the food delivery company. They sent me out in a hire van with a useless tail lift as it could only be operated from ground level (most either have buttons in the back of the truck within reach of the lift, or a remote box with a long wire that can be used from the ground or the higher level of the lift when raised). The flaps were non-existent and, as I had to be at ground level, I had no way of holding the cage. Once it decided to move (bear in mind I was parked on the flat this time) there was nothing I could do but stand well out of the way and let it fall. The chef came out and we had a good laugh about it, the only real damage was to my ego, but the eggs were broken, the flour punctured, the cream and yoghurt were everywhere. I took the van back and told them I wouldn't be using it again as it was unsafe and not fit for purpose.

By now, I had been back at this company for a couple of months and hated every minute of it. I was earning rubbish money through the agency and didn't like the lack of job security. I always imagined agency work to be free and easy in that I could please myself where and when I worked, but the reality was obviously nothing like this. They must have liked me though because I got offered a full time, permanent position with them. This offered me some security and a decent wage so, against my better judgment, I accepted. The transport manager assured me I'd easily earn £25k a year, no nights out involved, and all the company benefits. I figured at least it would give me some experience using my Class 2 licence and I'd get a decent reference out of it. Most employers needed you to hold a Class 2 licence for 2 years before giving you a job. They claim it's due to the insurance but I think it's another back-covering exercise.

My first few weeks as a full time employee seemed to be going well. I was assured I wouldn't be dropped into doing a round I didn't know and they proved this by sending me out for a couple of weeks with the regular drivers to learn their routes. They were both going on holiday soon and I'd be covering for them. The only problem that became apparent was that the wages were crap. Despite being promised a decent wage, I'd be lucky to earn any more than £17k a year. Wages were dependent on the amount of drops delivered and the amount of miles driven. This system was awful and completely unfair. After covering a couple of runs while the regular drivers were on holiday, I soon found out how unfair. One route was averaging 30 drops a day, but there were not many miles driven. The other run averaged 20 drops but, because the drops were far apart, the money was about £90 more a week. All this for less physical work. Despite being told I'd earn roughly £25k a year, the reality was that I was earning no more than £17k. It was time to move on, I despised the place and couldn't stand it any longer.

It is the only job I have ever handed my notice in to without having another lined up, that's how bad it was.

My last day was really good, one of those that is simply unbeatable. The transport manager thought I was leaving on the Wednesday, but my last day was actually on the Thursday so they had booked an agency driver for the day to cover my run and, instead of sending him home, he was sent out with me. It was his first day, and my last, so I probably wasn't the best person to give this poor lad my opinions about the company.

We had 30 drops in Nottingham and we started well, getting the 5 city centre drops delivered in good time. We headed out to drop number 6, a nursing home. No problem, cage delivered, empty loaded back on, strap secured, door shut. My second man did mention that the strap looked a bit frayed but it was well secured and we could check it at the next drop, which was only a short distance away.

On arrival at the next drop, we went round to the rear of the lorry and lowered the tail lift. I opened the shutter and, as soon as it was open 2 inches, I could see cream trickling out. Oops, this doesn't look good! With the shutter now fully open, we could see the full scale of the devastation within. The strap had snapped, sending 3 fully loaded cages flying. There was food everywhere. Flour, cream, dried soup, you name it. We looked at each and all we could do was laugh. We laughed for about 5 minutes, until it hurt, until we couldn't laugh anymore. The agency lad got down on his hands and knees and started to clean up the mess, still chuckling. I saw my opportunity and stamped on a small cream pot that was next to him, splattering his arm. The next thing I saw was a tub of yoghurt whizzing past my head! Thankfully, we stopped at that as a food fight in the back of a fully loaded lorry could last days.

We decided that the only course of action was to head back to the yard to clean up and try again. We re-secured the cages, properly this time, and I jumped out of the back, leaving the agency lad to close the shutter. Unfortunately, the tail lift was half down and covered in cream and assorted food stuff, and the poor lad slipped whilst pulling the shutter and ended up sliding under the rear of the lorry. He was ok, but had hurt his wrist as he went.

We headed back to the yard and one of the office staff took him to hospital. The transport manager told me that they would restack the cage and give the back of the truck a clean, if I wouldn't mind taking it back out for the rest of the deliveries. I did mind and told him I was off home. That was that, I never went near the place again. The transport manager caught up with me outside, asking for my security card back, just as I was about to post it down a drain! Luckily, he caught me in time. He lectured me that I should have left on better terms as I may need employment here again in the future. No thanks, I'd rather sleep in the gutter. I then lectured him on lying to prospective employees about the wages they would never have a chance of earning. 25K???

It probably sounds very childish leaving a job in that manner, and especially having a small food fight, but it was the letting off of steam that I sorely needed after working at this dreadful company for as long as I had!

The one saving grace of this job, apart from not being unemployed, was that some of the kitchens would give you a sandwich or fried egg bap. Also, I did learn some valuable life lessons from some of the old hands such as removing a chocolate bar from a box so nobody notices, or if you punch a big box of crisps in the right place, nine times out of ten, a bag can be removed, again, without detection.

Luckily, on my second to last day, whilst working my weeks' notice, I got a call from a company offering me a job. I had attended an interview a few weeks previously and had lost all hope of them getting back.

They said it had taken a long time to get references back but in real terms this means they took someone else on for the job who they thought would be better, it turned out that they weren't, so they are phoning me as I am second best. I wasn't complaining though as they had contacted me just at the right time and I could start on the Monday.

A NEW ROAD

This was to be one of the best jobs I have had. The money wasn't great, but the job made up for it. I would be delivering kidney dialysis fluids and equipment to hospitals and patient's homes across the country. The work was hard, a lot of lifting and carrying boxes upstairs, but there was never any resentment as the patient obviously couldn't do it for themselves. I was very lucky as, after only a couple of weeks, I was given my own route and my own lorry. Coincidentally, the driver who I was replacing had gone to work for the company I did the general haulage for previously. I wonder if he ever managed to lock himself out of the cab?

My route consisted of various 2 day runs to London, Bolton, Kent, East Anglia and a fortnightly run to Cornwall, which turned into a 3 day run in the summer months as a lot of patients went there on holiday and needed their dialysis fluids delivered.

There was never any real drama with this job, it usually went very smoothly but the days could get a bit boring. I used to set off at 3 o'clock on a Monday morning so I could access a bay at the Royal Free Hospital in Hampstead before everyone else got there and parked in the way. After this, I would head to Barnet Hospital, then to 5 patients throughout north and east London. Once finished, I would head north on the M1 and park somewhere like Rothersthorpe services for about 2pm. I would then wait until 6 the next morning before heading back to the depot. Anyone who has ever spent more than a couple of hours at a service station will know that there is not much else to do except eat or sleep.

If you got back to the yard too early, management would realise that your run could be done in a day, and they'd give you more work to do, so best to wait it out down the road, and out of sight! Once back at the yard on the second day, all that was left to be done was to load the truck for the following day and go home. If my truck was dirty I would give it a wash, but that was every couple of weeks. Most weeks I had 2 days when I was home for 10am so it was like having a couple of days off which, to me, made up for being away early the day before and staying out all night.

A few months after I started, the company moved to a brand new premises, near Mansfield, 30 minutes up the motorway from the old depot. A lot of drivers were not happy as they lived close to the old depot and now had to travel a lot further to work. I had recently moved out of Nottingham so was only about 10 minutes down the road from the new place, so didn't mind as it shortened my journey time. The only problem for me now was that, apart from a fortnightly run to East Anglia, and another to Bolton, all my runs were to the south so I had to add an extra half hour onto each journey. This meant I had to be leaving the yard at 2.30 on a Monday morning to get to London, which meant getting up at 2 am. That's still the day before!! On more than one occasion I slept in my lorry in the yard on the Sunday night so I could just get up and drive off, instead of the palaver of driving to work first.

The new depot had been built 2 units down from another of their old depots, the idea being that eventually both depots would merge.

Every day there were 5 or 6 lorry loads of fluids that had to be moved from the old depot to the new, a 3 minute drive away. A local haulage company was used for this and someone once told me that it cost our firm £32k a year to get this done. After a few months it was decided by management that drivers coming back on their 2nd day would take a load each, thus saving the company money. It made good sense to me and we couldn't complain as we still got to go home early.

So, from now on, I would get back to the yard half an hour earlier on my 2nd day, load up, drive round to goods in next door, unload, move to goods out, load my lorry for the next day, and head for home. I was still at home for the same time and no-one could complain as I'd done my work. Other drivers weren't so happy and moaned about the extra workload so they decided to stay away until lunchtime, so all the work would be done by the time they arrived back. I never understood their logic. There was no real work involved, just 20 minutes of time (we were salaried so were getting paid anyway) and they too could still have finished early. I was never once asked to do more than one load. On the one occasion I arrived back in the yard at lunchtime, it took me an hour before I could reverse on to a bay as there were 12 lorries to 4 loading bays. They would have been better off getting back earlier than sitting in a queue waiting to load.

Delivery to some hospitals could often be fun! Cars would be parked everywhere, blocking access, pallets would have to be dragged for miles through corridors to the dialysis unit, sometimes the wait for the lift could be 10 minutes due to the shear amount of people around.

I used to make sure I was out of the Royal Free in Hampstead just before 6am. The size of my truck allowed it to be easily blocked in if another vehicle parked in the bay next to me. This drop was as easy as they get though, all the pallets were dropped on the loading dock for the porters to take up to the dialysis unit at a later time.

Barnet Hospital was the complete opposite, all 8 pallets had to be dragged through the hospital to the lifts, up 2 floors, and along another maze of corridors to their final resting place. Here, all the pallets would be stripped down and the contents stacked on the floor or on the shelves. This was ok once you got to know where everything belonged, and the nurses were very helpful. I had a love/hate relationship with this place. I would sometimes use the 'trade' lift and, if I was unlucky enough to enter after the porter had been in there with the hazardous waste bins on his way to the incinerator, it would stink. This was not helped by the fact that these lifts were also very hot and stuffy, so I would be gagging all the way up to floor 3. I would, more often than not, use the patient lifts and, seeing as it was early morning, they were generally empty. I swear these lifts didn't appreciate my custom as I would always get a static shock when I pressed the buttons. No-one else ever seemed to and I was the only one to be seen wrapping my jumper round my hand and jabbing the buttons as quickly as possible. On one occasion, I had finished my delivery and was on my way down in the lift to load the empty pallets into the lorry and get on my way. The lift stopped at the next floor down and a lady was pushed in on a bed. She was screaming in agony and was obviously about to give birth. Luckily she made it out of the lift in time and avoided an undignified, if not interesting, start to her new baby's life. There was a collective sigh of relief when the lift doors shut after that experience, I can tell you!

I had some great times running to Cornwall and loved it, especially at the end of summer when it was still warm but the roads were empty. I also have fond memories of reading Jamaica Inn whilst parked for the night on a pitch black and stormy Bodmin

Moor.

My Cornwall run consisted of another early start, 03:30, and a boring drive down the M1/M42 to pick up the M5. My first drop was a patient in Highbridge, just outside Weston-Super-Mare, then onto a dialysis unit in Taunton. From there, I had an occasional drop at Watchet on the north Devon coast. On my first run down this way, the roads were damp which made them quite slippery. I approached a sharp right-hand bend and could see a Mini hurtling towards me. The driver had attempted to take the bend too fast for the road conditions, lost grip, slid across the road and bounced off of my rear wheel, before careering across to the bank on his side of the road and ploughing straight into the back of a stationary car. I put my hazard lights on and went to check that everybody was alright. He was unhurt and said the usual, stupid things that people say in these circumstances; "I didn't think I was going that fast" or "I didn't think the road was slippery". I pondered out loud that maybe next time he would think differently. He seemed ok until I pointed out that, had I not been in the way to stop him and bounce him back to his side of the road, there was nothing stopping him from a very steep drop into the fields below. Absolutely nothing. No barrier, no kerb stones, no bank, nothing. I left my details and headed on my way.

At the Taunton Dialysis Unit, the loading door was at

the side and the best course of action was to reverse in, dog-legging around a kerb that stuck out to the right and stopping level with the store room door, on the left. On one occasion, I had delivered my load, packed the empty pallets away and was driving off to my next destination. I pulled away, steered left around the kerb, watching my mirror to check I had cleared the building. No problem, loads of room, but was that I saw falling in my mirror? I stopped and jumped out to check and, on closer inspection, it turned out that the side of the lorry had scraped along the overhanging roof of the dialysis centre, breaking the gutter and dislodging a few tiles. Bear in mind that I had been to this drop on numerous occasions in the past, it's scary how a lapse in concentration can still cause an error such as this to occur. Lesson learned though, and I put it down to experience.

I seemed to be learning a good few lessons over the time I had been driving. My mistakes were never down to complacency, though. An error in judgment, yes. But complacency or stupidity? No.

After Taunton, it was a straight run down the A30 to hospitals in Truro and Penzance. I used to be able to make it back to Exeter services for the night in my 10 hours of driving but this changed when a new dialysis unit opened in Bodmin. Thankfully, they were more than happy to let me park up outside for the night. The unit was only open on 3 days a week and was never open on the days I delivered there. I was trusted with a key and the alarm code, and was told to make use of the toilet and shower facilities. There was also a kitchen, complete with microwave, which they were kind enough to let me use.

"Help yourself to tea and biscuits"

It's lovely to be treated with that amount of respect and, obviously, I never abused their trust. Most people think lorry drivers are the lowest form of life, and treat them as such, but it is rarely true. I have met some truly dreadful truckers, but I have met truly dreadful people from all walks of life. Your profession doesn't make you that way, though.

Incidentally, the UK is one of the worst countries for treating truckers badly. A lot of warehouses and Regional Distribution Centres (RDC's) won't allow us to use the toilet. At some places, they demand you hand your keys in to them before they will start unloading, leaving the poor driver sat on a hard wooden bench for anything up to 4 hours in a hot room with no access to the canteen, and again, with no chance of using the bog! Haemorrhoids are common among drivers due to all the sitting and inactive lifestyle so I shouldn't really need to point out to you how uncomfortable a wooden bench or hard, cold, plastic seat could be for more than 15 minutes!

When the summer months came, my Cornwall run was extended to 3 days. I used to be able to get my regular drops delivered a day early which left the second day to deliver all the 'extras', running around campsites, hotels, bed and breakfasts, caravan parks etc. to deliver in anticipation of the patient's arrival. Day 3 was reserved for running back to the depot, though I did occasionally have a delivery to make if I had run out of time to do it on day 2.

I used to love this part of the job, but it could be stressful trying to find a delivery point. One such time saw me trying to find a bed and breakfast in Devon. I found the village, I found the road, but there was no way I could turn down there due to a stone wall either side of the road and round the corner, it was just too tight. "But the bin lorry manages to get down here" is a popular one drivers will often hear, along with "We've had bigger than that in here". When you are new to driving big vehicles, statements like this make you think you are doing something wrong and are somehow inferior, surely I should be able to manage if someone else has managed? But, the reality of it is that the person saying these things generally has no clue of what they are talking about and don't realise how big your vehicle actually is, so you learn to ignore them. It's all down to experience, again, and you soon learn, through trial and error, where you can and can't go. I explained to the patient's husband that I wouldn't be able to fit down his road and, thankfully, he drove his car out to meet me and loaded it up with a pallet load of boxes. He did look at the vehicle and say it was actually bigger than the lorry the bin men used. As I said, you have to judge these things for yourself.

On another trip, I was given the address of a farmhouse bed and breakfast in Cornwall. I found the way to the village that the address gave me using my trusty Cornwall map. I drove round, looking for a house name, or clue to where I needed to be. I stopped and asked a few locals if they knew where it was. Everyone directed me back up the same way as I had just come, so I took another look. Nope, I still couldn't find it. I managed to get the phone number for the owner so called him up for directions. He said "Before you come to the village, you'll go over a bridge, my track is the next turning on the right, immediately after this". Thanks, I knew exactly where he meant! Off I went, back into the village (which, by now, I had been through 4 times), over the little bridge, but the next right just went nowhere, it disappeared, and came to an abrupt end, in some trees. Not much hope of it being there. I phoned the farm again and the man said he would walk down the end of the track and wait for me. I drove down the road again, and there was the man, at the end of a track. I jumped out and found out this was the place. I had no idea it would be here, it just didn't add up to the directions I'd been given. The track was very narrow, with overhanging trees either side, and looked like it went into a field. Oh well, I managed to reverse in and get off the road and from there, I was able to drag the pallet to the house using my trusty pallet truck, as it was only a few hundred yards away, and the boxes weren't heavy. I had a nice chat with the husband and wife over a cup of tea, and mentioned that I still hadn't seen the bridge. He assured me that the bridge was just to the left, out of the gate. I said goodbye and closed up the tail lift. I turned left out of the gate, heading back to the main road, and lo and behold, there was the bridge!! There was no hump in the road, the only clue was a wall, 2 bricks high and covered in bushes and undergrowth. I had eventually found the bridge I had been searching for, and it only took me 2 and a half hours!

It was a hot day and I decided to head to a favourite overnight parking place of mine, the Windy Ridge Diner in Trerulefoot, not far from the Tamar Bridge. The facilities here were great. There was rarely any other lorries parked here, they had a decent shower and clean toilet facilities, and the food was outstanding. I am a rare breed: a vegetarian lorry driver, so I don't usually bother eating at truckstops or cafes on the road as the menu is often limited. I always carried a gas cooker and my dinner usually consisted of soup with added new potatoes and vegetables, or tinned curry with boil-in-the-bag rice. I was only cooking like this for a couple of nights a week so it never got boring. I have lived on these type of meals for a week at a time since, and I don't really get bored with it (though it does help if you vary the soup and vegetables a bit). It is preferable to the junk the service stations feed you which is overpriced, undercooked, often lukewarm, and always vile.

This particular night, I had eaten well in the restaurant and showered. I headed back to my lorry for a relaxing read of my book and an early night. A lorry pulled up right next to me and I assumed he was lonely as the rest of the lorry park was empty. Now, I'm not antisocial, I'll chat with anyone, but when you're in your truck, it's your living room and bedroom for the night, so I'm not that keen on sharing my evening with anyone else. Also, I'm not interested in talking to people for the sake of it, about work, or about nothing, or the weather.

Anyway, my new neighbour opened his window and started chatting away. He did most of the talking and, after a while, I noticed that after every sentence, he said the word "Wizzit". I assumed this was local dialect (Andover, he told me) for something like the Londoners would say "Innit" or Liverpudlians say "La" The more he talked, the more this strange word was spoken, and I wondered if it was a nervous thing (or he was possibly winding me up, but I doubt it). We were chatting away quite happily for a while, until he started telling me all about his relationship and how he'd been kicked out of the house by his girlfriend and was having to live in his lorry for the time being. The conversation continued and he told me his girlfriend had gone to the police and reported him for hitting her. He protested to me saying that he'd never hit her, how much he loved her and, "Well, it only happened the once, anyway"

Ok.

Goodnight.

I double checked the doors were locked and went to bed, remembering that this was the very reason I tried not to get into an elongated conversation with someone I didn't know.

The problem is though, is that I seem to attract oddballs. I was once approached at Kings Lynn lorry park by another lonely trucker. Bald, toothless, rubber-faced meathead, he told me I should be careful walking round the back of the lorries as some truckers, desperate for the toilet but with no facilities for miles, would do their business there. I thanked him (though it was hardly news to me, or anyone else, when you the see the piles of pooh in some truck parks and laybys, resplendent with a topping of loo roll, sticking up like the candles on a birthday cake), and he started talking to me, normally at first. He then started to tell me about his mate who had fitted a toilet seat to the back of the truck. When he needed the toilet, he would just fold it down and do his business, onto the ground below. I have no idea whether he was telling me the truth, or stringing me along, but I have always checked out the backs of lorries on the motorway in the hope of seeing a bog seat dangling there.

While we're on the subject, toilet facilities on the road are generally atrocious, not to mention being few and far between at times. Whilst working between Nottingham and Felixstowe docks, I have been forced to park up in a layby for the night and have been 'caught short'. In this emergency situation, there is nothing else for it but to close the cab curtains, and empty your bowels into a carrier bag. Not the most pleasant thing to do, but with the alternatives being either to soil yourself, or get out in the middle of a freezing cold night and expose your delicate parts in a layby, leaving it for some other poor sod to step in. You could try holding it in, but I think some damage may be done, as well as a lot of discomfort, if left overnight!

There is also the need to relieve your bladder in the night and, whether you are parked in a service station or lay-by, you probably won't want to get dressed in the middle of a freezing cold winter's night and find a toilet or pee up against a wheel. There is also the added risk of getting 'done-over' in a dark lay-by by some hood looking to steel your wallet or precious cargo. Enter 'Trucker's Tizer'. Bottles of this liquid can be seen from Sussex to Aberdeenshire, Suffolk to Cumbria, littering the grass verges and motorway hard shoulder. I have peed in a bottle many times (hint: always use a bit of bog roll or tissue to catch the drips, and watch out for a pressure build up, 'Wide

Mouth' bottles are usually better!) but always dispose of them in a bin. There is no need to lob a bottle out of the window or leave it for someone else to pick up.

One guy I met, at the horrid father-son outfit in Nottingham, had a very near-miss with a bottle of 'Trucker's Tizer'. He was instructed to take a Transit down to Leicester with a load. On the motorway he started feeling thirsty and reached around behind the driver's seat to see if there was anything there. He found a near-full 2 litre bottle of, what he assumed was, Tizer or Orangeade. He was just about to take a swig when, luckily (or unluckily, depending on what way you look at it), the smell hit him and he nearly threw up! Lesson learned, and nearly the hard way, don't drink anything that has been left lying about in a van or truck cab.

I pulled into Hartshead Moor services on the M62 late on a rainy, windy night and, after buying some supplies from the shop, decided to use the toilet. On entering the toilet, I saw a man on his hands and knees, peering under a locked cubicle door, obviously trying to watch the person on the other side. Thankfully, on this occasion, I wasn't desperate so about-turned and vacated the premises. This sort of behavior is sickening and I hope when these people get caught, they get everything they deserve.

The M5 services during the summer are generally worth avoiding too. On entering one of the cubicles, a kind caravanner had emptied their chemical toilet, but had missed the bowl completely and got most of it over the floor. To be honest, you'll be lucky to find the space to park a truck at this time of year as all the caravanners decide they have to take up space in the truck park as they simply can't park in 2 spaces in the car park. This leaves us with nowhere to park so we either have to park awkwardly (and possibly making it difficult for other large vehicles to enter and manoeuvre) or go somewhere else at the risk of running over our legal hours. GRRR!

Coming north one day on the M5, I saw a bad accident on the southbound carriageway. There was a stationary artic, a 7.5 tonne lorry on its side and a motorbike lying in the road someway ahead. I hoped that no-one had been hurt but, with a bike involved, it's probably wishful thinking.

A few weeks later I delivered to a courier that we used for deliveries that I wouldn't have time for, or that were too small for my lorry to get near to. I had got to know them quite well over the last year or so and, over a cup of tea, I found out it was their 7.5 tonne vehicle that was involved in the accident that day. I had met the driver a few times and luckily he was uninjured. He had been overtaking the artic when it veered into his lane. He took evasive action, lost control, and his vehicle ended up on its side. A good few minutes later, the motorbike struck the back of the 7.5 tonne vehicle and the rider was killed instantly.

Another patient I delivered to in Devon always left their door unlocked for me so I could sneak in quietly in the early morning and stack their delivery up in the living room. I had met the patient and her husband on a number of occasions and they were lovely people, very friendly and helpful. The husband would always bring his wheel barrow to my lorry so I didn't have to struggle and he would help me get the boxes to the house. They were both keen bikers, always going away on the bike for camping holidays. Some months later I found out he had been killed in an accident around the same time and often wondered if the events were linked. Very sad, it is a stark reminder that driving for work, and for pleasure, is a very dangerous undertaking and any one of us may not return home.

I enjoyed the job of kidney dialysis deliveries because it wasn't just a delivery job. The patients were (usually) happy to see you, a lot regarded us as their lifeline. This was apparent at Christmas when the tips would roll in: £10 here, bottles of wine and whisky there. All very much appreciated. One patient in Kent even gave me a present to take home for my daughter, which was lovely of them. A new patient started her dialysis in the London area and was added to my round. She was very nervous, felt alone, and didn't know anyone to speak about it with who would understand what she was going through. I used to talk to her about the difficulties some of my other patients had and she realised she wasn't alone.

I had only delivered to her a few times and was very touched when she gave me a Christmas tip and card that read "Thank you for all you have done for me". It felt like we were a small part of what these people were going through, rather than just someone who turns up with a delivery once a week.

My regular 2-day runs on Monday/Tuesday and Thursday/Friday were broken up with a day run on the Wednesday. This was often a few drops in Birmingham, but sometimes I would be given a run to Manchester or the Warrington area. It was Parent's Evening at my daughter's school on this particular day, which had me delivering to 7 patient's houses in Warrington, Runcorn and St Helens. I had done this run before and knew I should be back in good time that evening. We were still based in Long Eaton at that point so I thought the easiest route would be west on the A50 to pick up the M6 northbound. I got across the A50 with no problem, it was still only 6 in the morning as I had set off early to miss the traffic. As soon as I entered the slip road onto the M6, I knew there was a problem. The traffic was usually heavy at this time of the morning but today it was a lot slower. 2 miles up the road, we were at a standstill. Oh well, it should clear soon. How wrong I was! We were stationary for nearly 2 hours and, even after that, it was very slow going. There had been an accident on the Thelwall Viaduct and, though the road was now open again, traffic had built up so much that no-one was going anywhere fast for at least another hour or two.

I checked the map and figured it would be best to leave the M6 at junction 18 (A54 to Winsford) then north on the A49, picking up the A533 to my first drop in Runcorn. Traffic was very slow through Middlewich and Winsford but was almost at a standstill again once I turned onto the A49. It seemed a lot of other drivers had the same idea. I phoned one of the other drivers, who knew this run I was doing, and told him of my hold-up and that I was hoping to get home. He was delivering to the north of Manchester and then on to Liverpool and, out of the kindness of his heart, he said he would meet me at my second drop and take a couple of the drops from me and deliver them. It was always nice when another driver would help out and I always tried to repay the favour by lightening their load by a drop or two at some point. With him taking the extra load off me, I was able to complete my run and get back for the Parent's Evening.

Things rarely go as planned on the road and this was no more evident than one wintry Sunday when I set off for my usual drops in Norfolk, following the coast to the north and delivering to Wells-Next-The-Sea, Sheringham, Cromer, North Walsham and finishing up in Great Yarmouth where I would sometimes park up for the night in the lorry park or, more often than not, I would get some of the homeward journey out of the way and finish my day in King's Lynn. This particular day was different in that it was between Christmas and New Year. Deliveries were all over the place as the firm shut down for the 25th, 26th and 1st but people still needed their dialysis fluids (and probably wouldn't appreciate it turning up when they are just about to sit down to their Turkey) so a number of us were asked if we could work on the Sunday to catch up. I said yes as I had already had 2 days off (paid) and the Sunday would be paid at double time. The patients on my route had been asked if they would accept a Sunday delivery and all had obliged, all that would remain would be for me to run back in to the yard on the Monday morning.

I set off on the long, boring road to King's Lynn. The day was ice cold with a bitter wind and some snow lingered at the sides of the road. Still, there was no traffic to be seen and I made good time getting to my first drop in Wells. I arrived and knocked on the door, and headed back to my lorry to lower the tail lift. The tail lift on our fleet was also the back door so, when the tail lift was in the closed position, it was just one big metal flap that covered the back of the truck. It was a good system as, when it was lowered, there were no back doors to open and secure in position. The tail lift was big enough to get 2 loaded pallets, a pallet truck, and the driver on. It had 2 big foot buttons fitted so the driver only had to press these to move up or down, leaving their hands free, as well as levers fitted to the side of the truck body for operation from the ground (mainly used for closing it).

On this occasion, I attempted to lower the tail lift. Nothing. Hmmm…..I tried again. Still nothing. The power was not getting to the lift. I checked in the cab that the tail lift power button was switched to the 'ON' position. It was. I tried waggling the levers again. Still nothing. In situations like these (and, being a truck driver, there are many) it is sometimes something simple that has been overlooked so it is a bit of a shock when you realise that there is nothing that you can do to fix the situation. Also, you ponder as to whether it is something simple that you have missed and how stupid you will look when the garage mechanic comes out, flicks a switch, calls you a twat, and drives off again. Still, on this day, I was confident that I hadn't missed anything and it just was not working.

I phoned my office (one of the staff had taken the mobile phone home just in case of emergencies) and told them the problem. They said they would contact a local garage to come and take a look. They then called back 5 minutes later to say the garage would be about an hour. I told the patient what the problem was, and sat in my warm cab and waited. Just over 2 hours later, a white van pulled up and out jumped a mechanic. He checked to see if there was power getting to the motor, which there was, so he deduced that the motor wasn't working. He removed it and stripped it down, replacing the brushes and some of the connectors. Once the motor was re-fitted, the tail lift worked perfectly. This had taken about half an hour (in the freezing cold), but I was able to finally deliver my first load of the day.

Onwards I went to my second drop at Sheringham. I pulled up in the road, some way away from my delivery point as there were parked cars everywhere (and, having delivered to this road many times, and been blocked in on more than one occasion, was very wary and stayed out of the way round the corner). I set about lowering the tail lift and, when it had tilted open approximately 2 foot, the motor made a funny whirring noise and the whole thing went silent. Bloody hell! I tried moving the levers again, nothing. I went to the house I was delivering to and explained the situation and that it was the second time today it had happened, hence why I was late. They were pretty easy going so I left them in their warm house and headed back to my cab to phone the office again. Same as before, about an hour and a half later, a van turned up (a different company this time). I told him what the problem had been at the first call out and he immediately removed the motor and stripped it down. It was burnt out. He didn't have a spare motor on him, or at his garage, but could order one. I told him not to bother as it would be easier for someone to come out to the depot back in Mansfield to fit one the following day. He re-secured the motor and headed away, but not before manually closing the tail lift for me.

There was nothing left for me to do than turn round and head for home and, by now, I was getting very cold (with one of those nice snotty noses you get from standing around in the cold for longer than is healthy) and very hungry. My sandwiches had been eaten waiting for the first mechanic to arrive. I phoned the office again, and told them I was heading back and would be back in the morning when, hopefully, they could get someone out with a new motor to fix the problem.

Hoping for some hot food and a nice cup of tea, I parked up at the services near Long Sutton. The time was now 6.25pm and they had closed at 6. Still, I had some tins and my trusty cooker so set about making some dinner. The night heater was then fired up whilst I watched a DVD in the cosy warmth of my cab before turning in for the night.

This day must have cost my company an absolute fortune. 12 and a half hours (at double time) in wages. 2 garage call-outs. Fuel from Mansfield to Sheringham and back again, all to deliver to one patient. On top of that, the other 4 drops that I was carrying would still need to be delivered and the tail lift would need fixing!

I held this job for just under 2 very enjoyable years, but my circumstances were changing, along with the management, so I decided to quit while I was ahead and look for something different. This was a hard decision, but in the end I knew it was the right thing to do. It was difficult telling some of the patients I was leaving, especially those I had known for a long time. I often think about some of them, especially when I travel to different areas of the UK, or when I'm feeling reflective and wonder how they are doing, whether they still live in the same place or, sadly, if they are still alive.

As I have mentioned more than a few times, the original dream was to obtain my Class 1 licence but I had pretty much decided against it as it looked too difficult. The more I heard, and saw every day on the roads, the more this was the best course of action. Stick with what I was doing. Having got in a few scrapes and sticky situations in a rigid lorry, the risk of getting stuck in a bendy artic became even more apparent. You could drive into somewhere and actually get stuck as the physics of reversing it are different to moving forward. Any place you could get in with a rigid, however tight or awkward, you can always reverse out the same way. Nope, no thanks, I'm sticking with the easy option.

DIZZY HEIGHTS

In 2004, I decided to look into how much my Class 1 licence would cost to acquire. A 5 day intensive course, with the test on the 5th day, would be somewhere in the region of £980. Add this to the £920 my Class 2 licence cost, it soon adds up.

By now, I was working for a local company mainly doing day runs, delivering steel to building sites. There was quite a bit of distance involved, but not too many nights out. The hourly rate of pay was good, so working long hours gave me a good wage at the end of each week. They had taken me on as a Class 2 driver and, after I had worked there for a few months (to prove myself), they would pay to put me through my Class 1 test. This seemed great to me as, despite not really wanting to drive these big, scary lorries, if someone else was paying, I'd be stupid not to seize the opportunity.

The job seemed pretty good and I settled into it well. It became obvious that I didn't get on with the boss's son (what is it with the boss's son? Something to do with privilege?). This made me reconsider getting caught up with this firm for a year or however long they wanted to keep hold of me to make their investment pay. Some people say that a firm can't hold you to anything as it's considered training necessary for the job, but there are probably ways round this. One lad had managed to get this company to pay for his licence and he was never seen again, rumour has it he moved back down to London. I'm not like that, I'd rather pay my own way and not rip someone off. So that's what I decided to do. I managed to scrape the money together using some of my wages and some from the credit card, figuring I'd be able to pay it off once my 'rock star' wages from driving a proper big rig came rolling in.

The company were not happy when, a few months later, I declined their offer to start my training. I got a phone call one Friday telling me to bring my driving licence into the office on Monday. I asked why (as they only checked it at my interview 3 months previous) and I was told I'd be starting my training at the end of the next week.

I started enquiring at some local training schools, and managed to book a test drive with one. This would cost me £30 (I'm not sure why I paid this, it certainly seems like a rip off now writing it down on paper!) and in that time they would assess my driving skills and tell me how long they thought I would need. It was probably worth the money to see what it's like to actually drive an articulated vehicle. I arranged to go along the following afternoon for a drive.

I turned up and was kept waiting by the boss man who was on the phone. He then told me to take a seat as the instructor would be back shortly. After 45 minutes, the instructor came in and, with no apology or acknowledgment that I had been waiting ages, handed me the keys and told me to "Get in the cab". I instantly disliked the man. I did get a good 40 minute drive round town, but when he started making racist comments about a family of Asians walking across the road, I knew I wouldn't be spending 5 days in this seat with him. Yet another one of the lowlifes we meet, this time he assumed I was too.

I resumed my search of local instructors but didn't like the look of any of them. There was nothing essentially wrong with them, but they all used flatbed rigid trucks pulling a flatbed trailer (this combination is called a drawbar). This was unacceptable to me as my first day driving would be in a proper articulated truck so I wanted to learn what it would be like to pull a full size, high trailer. A flatbed gives better rear vision and would be easier on the reversing test, but I didn't want to make life easy, I wanted to learn the hard way.

I found a company that used a Scania unit coupled to a 40ft refrigerated box trailer. This was ideal. I was used to a Scania, having driven one for 2 years. The gearbox would take some getting used to if you had never driven one before, but I was comfortable with it.

This particular gearbox has eight gears. 1st, 2nd, 3rd and 4th gear are in the same position as you would find in most cars, utilising the 'H' pattern. A switch is then flicked into the 'up' position on the side of the gear lever and, as soon the lever is in the neutral position, a small 'clunk' can be heard which tells the driver that top range is selected. 1st gear position now becomes 5th, 2nd gear 6th and so on. The opposite technique is used when gearing down, by flicking the range change to the down position. Another switch on the lever 'splits' every gear which, in effect, gives you 16 gears to use. Splitting gears is only used when loaded and when changing a whole gear will be too much.

If you are not used to this style gearbox, it could well be confusing, especially combined with driving a bigger vehicle than you are used to AND being in the stressful situation of lessons or a test. My instructor told me that some people can take a couple of days just getting used to changing gear which is time that could otherwise be used learning the basic manoeuvres. One of the biggest problems is not knowing which gear you're in. Another is that if you try to change into high range or low range too quickly, the gearbox will just stay in neutral, you have to take a bit of time and do everything slowly to avoid this. Not easy at times, as I found out a few years earlier. I was driving a fully loaded rigid lorry up a steep hill in Derbyshire and needed to change from 5th to 4th. I flicked the switch into low range, and changed gear quickly as I didn't want to lose too much speed. The box went into neutral, I couldn't retrieve any gear at all, so all I could do was stop (much to the frustration of the cars behind), select first gear, and start again! It's called learning the hard way and there's lots more of that to come, you get used to it after a while.

I arrived for my assessment and found the instructor to be friendly, well turned-out (his vehicles and his clothes) and the whole outfit looked professional. We had a look round the vehicle and he ran through some of the things that would be required of me in the test. This included dropping the trailer and hitching it back up again, checking the vehicle over and having to answer questions about checking the oil and water (but not having to actually show the examiner). Then we were in the cab, with me in the passenger seat and the instructor (from now on known as Paul) driving. We pulled over on a quiet road and I was instructed to climb into the hot seat and, I don't mind admitting, I was very nervous at this point. He ran through the basics of the vehicle followed by some gear changing exercises. I did well on this and it was decided I would need 4 days of training, with the test on the 5th day. I decided this time that I wanted one-on-one training as, although I had enjoyed sharing the cab with Steve when learning to drive a rigid, I felt that driving a class 1 may require longer behind the wheel. Paul was worried that things might get very intense due to not being able to get a break from being behind the wheel, but I was ok with this.

I was booked in for three weeks' time, starting on the Wednesday. I would learn all day Wednesday, Thursday and Friday, take the weekend off, resume lessons on the Monday with my test booked in for the Tuesday. I wasn't keen on this idea as I wanted to get the whole thing over and done with in one block, thinking that if I took the weekend off, I might forget some of the things I had been taught the previous week and would have to (almost) start again on the Monday morning and, with the test the following day, I wouldn't have enough time to get back up to speed. As it was, I was completely wrong. The course was very intense and I was extremely glad to get the weekend off to relax.

I booked the 5 days off work, and the Wednesday couldn't come soon enough. I also had visions of telling my boss, in no uncertain terms, where to stick his job just before disappearing into the sunset in a big rig! I'd be my own boss on the open road, no-one was going to tell me what to do. If I didn't like the job I was doing, I would be able to walk out and start another on the following Monday. Then I decided I should probably ground myself in reality and get the lessons and, more importantly, the test, out of the way first before jumping too far ahead of myself.

Wednesday morning came and I was nervous as hell! I had even been taking 'Kalms' tablets for the week leading up to this point to see if they'd help, I'm not sure how bad I'd have been if I hadn't. I was also excited but, with all that money at stake, it seemed like a big gamble and the pressure was on to pass. I'm sure it's the same for everyone though. It would cost me £980 if I passed 1st time. If I failed, another test plus refresher lessons would be another £300 on top, and the more time that passed between lessons, the more chance there was of failure due to being out of practice. I could barely afford the fee in the first place, let alone any additional costs. The pressure was definitely on!

Every morning the procedure was the same. Arrive at 8am and have a chat over a coffee. This was always about what the test would hold, or the previous day's highlights or balls-ups. Then we would head out to where the unit was parked, via the toilet (coffee + nerves), where we would check the oil and water levels, the lights and the tyres. We would then hop in and drive round to where the trailer was parked. Next, I would reverse the unit up to the trailer, stopping just short of it. Then, I would exit the cab and check the 5th wheel* height against the trailer, as well as checking the trailer park brake is on. This will be a red button located somewhere on the chassis on the side of the trailer, and can be found in all manner of places. Some are at the rear on the driver's side, others are halfway along (on either side) or at the front on the passenger side. Or anywhere else, you'll have to hunt for it yourself as all trailers are different. Make sure you have a torch in your kit as it will typically be dark when you need to locate it. Some trailers do have a sticker on the body to identify the location though, which is handy. Once found, pull it out to engage the brakes, push in to release**.

After checking the height of the 5th wheel (it will always be ok when you're using the same unit and no-one else is using the trailer) it's time to reverse the unit underneath until the pin clicks securely in place. Once clicked in, 1st gear is selected and the unit 'tugged' forwards twice*** to make sure the locking mechanism is securely in place.

Time to put some gloves on and jump out of the cab again. I say 'jump', I mean 'exit the cab in a safe fashion making sure that 3 points of contact are kept with the unit handrails/steps at all times'. Incidentally, as a youngster, I used to watch a lot of truckers (the bin men/delivery drivers etc.) and they would always open the cab door and leap out. Do drivers still do this? I don't, though I have done on a couple of occasions. Maybe it's due to the increased height of cabs these days? Jumping out of a Daf XF cab would be akin to leaping off a small skyscraper. I did read about one such driver a number of years back who, leaping from his cab whilst holding onto the door, managed to catch his wedding ring on the handle and ripped a finger off. Not nice. Not too good for your knees either, I hear.

Anyway, once safely on terra firma, it's time to secure the dog clip on the 5th wheel in place. This is to stop the 5th wheel release lever from jumping out of position and the unit parting company with the trailer half way down the A38. Don't worry though, it's just a safety precaution. Also, if you can't get the dog clip to fit through the hole, the trailer is probably not connected properly so you might want to start again.

Next up are the susies****. These are air lines and power lines that will connect your unit to your trailer so you have brakes and lights, consisting of 2 airlines (red and yellow), 2 electrical connections and a trailer ABS line.

Once all this is done, wind the legs up. The handle may be hard to turn on older trailers (or if loaded and the legs are still on the ground). Make sure you stow the handle back in its clip/holder. You're nearly ready to go, it's just a matter of securing the number plate onto the trailer (clips into place) and releasing the park brake, all the while checking the trailer sides for damage, collision rails for damage/security, tyres, wheel nuts and lights. By the way, it's hard to tell if a wheel nut is loose as they won't be loose to the feel. Just check that there are no rust lines streaking out of them towards the tyres and that there is no shiny clean metal around them. If there is either of these, best to get them re-torqued as a truck wheel running amok can do serious damage and can kill.

Driving an articulated vehicle for the first time is a very odd experience. I had never driven with a caravan or trailer in the past, so was a complete novice at anything that bends when going round a corner. Every bend that you encounter, every obstruction, one question comes to mind: "Can I make it through there?" Even though a junction can be wide, it's sometimes hard to see a route through. Still, it's best to be cautious to start with (and indeed to never get complacent regardless of how many years you've been driving). These vehicles could easily kill a pedestrian without the driver even knowing it, if all reasonable precautions aren't taken i.e. use your mirrors, use your mirrors and USE YOUR MIRRORS! Not to mention that there is absolutely no shame in stopping, and getting out for a look, if you're really not sure. Better that than wiping out a parked car, regardless of how much of an idiot the driver is for parking in such a stupid position. A car could run into the back of your trailer without you even feeling a bump, that's how big and tough these lorries are. As I've said, the mirrors are one of the most important safety features for a driver. Most lorries have a very useful blind spot mirror fitted on both doors (though some still just have one on the passenger side). This mirror, as well as being useful to check for cars alongside that wouldn't be visible in the normal mirror, is extremely useful to see where the back of your trailer is on a tight corner, again, when it's out of the range of the standard mirror. Most trucks have a 'kerb' or 'parking' mirror on the passenger door which, you've guessed it, gives a view downwards to the front wheel and kerb. Again, this is useful for seeing how close to a kerb or white line the truck is, but is also useful to see if a cyclist or pedestrian has sneaked down the side whilst waiting at traffic lights. A lot of new lorries are now fitted with another mirror, located just above the windscreen which gives a view of the road immediately ahead of the front bumper which, again, would otherwise not be visible to the driver. I am 6ft 3 inches yet, if I walked in front of a lorry, the driver would have no idea I was there as the bottom of the windscreen is still a foot or so above my head so this one is very useful when driving around towns and cities. This mirror, along with the kerb mirror, will be irreplaceable when manoeuvring around a tight yard when every inch of space counts and getting as close to that pile of discarded pallets could mean the difference in getting round the corner or having to reverse back and starting again. Despite all these mirrors, there are still a ridiculous amount of blind spots to be aware of, some that will even be big enough to 'lose' a car in.

This is why it is imperative to be on guard at all times and, if in doubt, stop and get out for a look.

Every part of a lorry is a hazard, the vision, the weight, trailer overhang (which can swing out when turning), the trailer headboard (front of the trailer) will also swing out when cornering, and all these dangers have to be taken into account. It can be a lot to take in for the new driver, but will become second nature over time.

My first day of lessons was spent getting used to the vehicle. We started out on some large A roads, before heading into the tighter roads of Nottingham. When driving in a straight line, the lorry is no wider than the rigid vehicles I was used to driving. The full size of the vehicle is felt when cornering or pulling out at junctions and roundabouts. Everything has to be done slowly and smoothly, but with enough speed to keep the flow of traffic moving. I have known numerous (rigid/artic/coach) drivers that have failed to pass their test due to hesitating, or pulling out in front of a car, at a roundabout. I always thought that this was particularly unfair as some of these drivers gave an otherwise good drive but fell at this hurdle. Take for example: a car driver is approaching a roundabout from the right. The car is actually turning left but does so without indicating. If you were to stop and wait for him, you could be construed as hesitating in the eyes of some examiners. Likewise, if a car comes hurtling round from the right, and you are already moving as the road was clear when you committed yourself to moving out, it could be seen as pulling out in front of the them. Taking into account the size, and slowness, of a full-size articulated truck starting from a stop, it's a wonder any of us actually get through the test with a pass mark. Both of the examples above could be marked down as a fault (if they add up to 15 it's a fail) or, if more serious, a definite fail. A lot of these are variable from examiner to examiner and seem a bit unfair but I was lucky with my examiners so can't complain.

My nearest HGV test centre was in Nuttall, on the outskirts of Nottingham, so I spent a lot of time driving on some of the test routes. They ranged from country roads and motorways to inner city driving which gave me good all round practice. My instructor was a funny little man with greasy, black hair. He was always very smartly dressed and I think that the starch from his shirts had rubbed off on him a few too many times. He seemed very jumpy, which is not what you need when nervous yourself, and he was constantly barking orders. I mean constantly. He would give a barrage of orders, some of which came so thick and fast that it was hard to complete one without starting another or forgetting what he had said. Then, once the manoeuvre was successfully executed he would say something like "Look at that, that's perfect, great job!" Meanwhile, I was left wondering exactly what it was that I'd done so well, and how the hell did I managed to do it due to being talked through every square inch of the road? It also left me wondering why the hell I had plumped for this bloody one-on-one tuition in the first place when there could have been someone else for him to shout at and take some of his abuse. I didn't really take it to heart but certainly wouldn't recommend him to anyone of a nervous disposition. He also used to come out with some odd phrases like

"Top banana!" or "Now, that's trucking in the real world" (when you'd managed to complete a turn that was harder than any they tested you on, for example) which I found both amusing and tiresome. My favourite of his was FU***NG SPIDERS!!!

I was very amused with one of his stories he told me. An older guy had booked in for a refresher course as he hadn't driven for a number of years. They went on an assessment run and ended up driving along the A1. Something went awry with the driving (I can't remember what it was, maybe the driver breathed on the windscreen in the wrong manner?) but it culminated in Paul leaping across to the driver's side (no doubt releasing a cry of "FU***NG SPIDERS!!"), wrestling the wheel out of the old guy's hand, and attempting to bring the rig to a controlled stop in a layby. A word of advice: DO NOT become a driving instructor of any size vehicle, be it bus, artic or car, if you are a nervous passenger, take an overly amount of anal pride in your wagon, or are just highly strung. Unfortunately for me, Paul was all three!

So, back to the lessons. Usually around 4.30pm we headed back to base and would park the trailer into its overnight resting place. This involved a 90 degree reverse into a narrow road, made more difficult by having a fence directly to the left of the cab which hindered any attempt to turn too tightly. On one occasion, we arrived back at the usual time, and I pulled up into position ready to reverse the trailer round. If you can imagine, the fence is to my left and the road I'm about to reverse into, is behind me on the right. I selected reverse gear and proceeded to reverse back, with a gentle left-hand turn on the steering wheel which would slowly start to bring the trailer round to the right. I was happily doing this, the trailer was turning nicely, but was aware that my passenger side mirror was only about a 10 inches away from the fence. I was crawling very slowly at this point so it was easy enough to check both mirrors for trailer position and the closeness to the fence. All of a sudden, my instructor starts screaming and nearly jumps out of his seat! I hit the brakes and stop immediately, thinking there is a huge problem (such as a car pulling up in my blind spot). He starts yelling about his mirror and how much it would cost to replace. He had been so busy checking the driver's side mirror, watching where the trailer was going, that he hadn't even glanced at the passenger mirror and, on looking up, he must have seen the fence and how close the mirror was. I told him that this was rubbish and that I had been checking both mirrors and was well aware of exactly how close I was to the fence. I did convince him in the end, but it took 4 attempts. I had driven the exact same cab with the exact same mirrors in the past (albeit in rigid form), so knew exactly how wide it was and was used to reversing into tight spaces and close to walls etc. I didn't like the fact that he seemed to think that none of his pupils had ever driven a lorry before, despite knowing full well that any of us training for our Class 1 licence would already have to hold a Class 2. If all this was true and we were either useless or had never driven a truck before, why wasn't HE checking both mirrors as he was the instructor and obviously far more experienced than the rest of us???

Day 2 saw the usual routine of coffee, toilet and coupling up, but instead of heading out onto the road, we went onto the local disused airfield. This was the part I was dreading the most. This was the very reason I never, ever wanted to become an artic driver. This was the spine-tingling reversing exercise! Rigid lorries were nice and easy (in comparison), just like a car, if you turned the steering wheel to the right, the back of the vehicle would turn to the right. Simple. Not with an artic though. If you turn the steering wheel to the right, the trailer will turn to the left. For the novice, this does actually take some thinking about. I understood the principle but, in practice, it was just confusing. I remember on family holidays as a child, my dad attempting to reverse into a parking space with our small trailer, deciding after a couple of attempts that it would be easier to get my mum to unhitch it and park it by hand. This wasn't really an option for a 42ft trailer.

The first exercise I performed was the straight reverse. Exactly as it says, attempting to reverse in a straight line. This is not part of the test, but it is great practice and a good way to start to get your head around 'opposite lock' and 'pivot points'. It basically consisted of driving to the end of the airfield and reversing to the other end. There was a seam in the concrete, which was useful to follow. As you reverse, you check both mirrors constantly and the idea is that if you see more of the trailer in one mirror than the other, you are not going in a straight line, so need to gently steer in that direction to correct it and straighten the trailer. Trying to steer in smooth, small movements was the first problem. My first attempt was very poor, swinging from side to side, weaving all over the place, over-steering and over-correcting with each movement. This is the basic 'newbie' mistake, and takes a long while to break the habit of. My second attempt went a lot better and Paul decided I was now ready for the feared reversing exercise.

As with the Class 2 exercise, the vehicle had to be reversed out of one coned box, across diagonally into the other box and stopped with the rear of the trailer in the correct place. Only this time, the vehicle was longer, bendier, and with a lot less vision and the boxes were obviously set further apart.

I set off on my first attempt, talked through the process by Paul. It didn't actually go too badly, though I did struggle turning into the second box. Pulling up at the cones in the first box posed no problem, and I was fine reversing out and turning to the left to head towards the second box, but I wasn't sure when to straighten up so I'd be in the correct position for the turn into box 2. This is when things started getting a little heated and my palms started to sweat. After a good few attempts I definitely improved, but was nowhere near good enough to be confident. Paul didn't really help much, to be honest. He would hop out of the cab and insisted that he would just watch me, without saying anything, so I could get the hang of it for myself. So I would then set off, with him standing outside, silently, watching my every move like a hawk. I would reverse out fine, turn the wheels (missing the cones at the side with the cab), straighten up, and head for the second box. He would still be silent at this point, though must have been biting his lip, as he would suddenly explode, shouting orders at me, telling me what I was doing wrong, or how to do it right! I would have been better off if he'd left me to it and would have eventually worked it out for myself, which would leave it imprinted on my brain. I am a firm believer that people will learn by their own mistakes and, sometimes, this is the best course of action. Paul didn't. He told me of a fellow instructor that allowed his pupils to get on with it alone, once they'd been shown the basics, while he went off for a cup of tea. How I wish I'd chosen this other instructor to teach me. Paul thought the guy was a brave man (for leaving the trainees alone with his precious truck) and mad (because there was no way they could learn anything without an expert present to shout orders to them or tell them what they were doing wrong). This was how my Class 2 instructor worked and he'd leave us to it, heading off for the last hour to tidy his paperwork etc. It was great for us to work it out for ourselves. On the test, you can use the mirrors or lean out of the window to reverse, it didn't matter, you could remove your seatbelt for this too, but I was told to ONLY use the mirrors, it was a pride thing as my instructor couldn't lose face in front of the other instructors. It would have made life easier, but it was good to learn the hard way.

**ARTICULATED LORRY MANOEUVRE
(NOT TO SCALE)**

Left a bit, right a bit. No! NO!

?

Next up on the airfield was the braking exercise and gear change exercise. These were covered when taking the Class 2 test, but still needed to be practiced. The purpose of the gear change exercise is to prove to the examiner that you can use every gear in the box (all 8, but you don't have to split gears) going first up through the box, then down again. This is because most of the time, with an empty trailer, you rarely use some of the gears and 'block change' up and down. It's different from driving a loaded artic as you would generally start off in 1st gear if it was very heavy, but when empty you only need 2nd gear, or even 3rd, to get started. I usually use 2nd to 4th, then 5th, 6th, 7th and 8th. It all depends on the road ahead, inclines etc. So, this was just to prove you knew how the whole gearbox worked.

Monday came around very quickly after a relaxing weekend off and I enjoyed my time away from Paul. I was dreading starting back on the Monday, not to mention the test looming rapidly on the horizon. Today was a lot more intense, going over and over everything I had learned, with particular focus on the downhill start. I had never had to do this before so needed to spend more time on this than any of the other manoeuvres (except for reversing, obviously). The downhill start started, amazingly, by stopping on a downward sloping hill. After the 'mirror, signal, manoeuvre' routine, 3rd gear is selected. With the clutch down, the footbrake is pressed and the handbrake released. The footbrake is then released but with the clutch still depressed so, in effect, you were now 'coasting'. Once enough speed has been gained, the clutch is then slowly lifted and then, after rolling for a few metres more, acceleration is applied and the vehicle driven away as normal. This was all a bit odd as, at any other point in the test, you would fail for cruising with the clutch down, and would be deemed 'not in full control of the vehicle'. But here I was, with a 44-tonne artic, hurtling into oblivion with no gears. A bit dramatic, but hypocritical all the same. It also annoyed me that Paul had left this gem until the day before my test, deciding this would be the best time to show me something completely new that I would need to learn. It's not that difficult, but it still needs to get into your head.

That night, I didn't sleep well at all, going over everything in my head a thousand times. Soon enough, it was morning. I arrived at the usual time and, with coffees drank and recycled, the unit checks were done. On this occasion I noticed something out of place which, on further inspection, turned out to be a suspension arm that had detached itself from its bracket and was trailing on the ground. I pointed this out to Paul and, on closer investigation, the securing bolt was missing. This was test day and, if there was no vehicle to take the test in, I was screwed. I'll give Paul his due though, as he rolled up his sleeves and donned his boiler suit (covering his pristinely pressed suit) and scrabbled under the vehicle to investigate further. He disappeared into his office to phone a parts supplier for a new strut as the hole at the end of this one was worn due to the loose bolt. The parts supplier couldn't get a new strut to him until the next day, but were rushing out a new bolt so we could at least get on the road. This would be about an hour, so I repeated the coffee and toilet ritual a few times and decided to have a wander round the warehouse in which his office was situated. I had spoken to the warehouse lads already so they knew who I was and stopped for a chat to pass the time. I stopped next to some very large boxes which, I found out, contained coffins. One of the lads removed a box so I could see inside. They were of the huge American variety, garishly white, like the ones you see in the movies, covered in brass rails and handles. The transport company got them shipped from America and attached all the brass work to them, fitting them with plush velvet linings, and delivering them to funeral directors around the country, most of these being in the London area. The caskets cost a fortune to be buried in and some people think they look the business (though I personally think they look tacky) but, if you inspect them closely, the insides are made from chipboard with a hardwood veneer on the outside. For their weight, as well as cost, I would have thought they would be made from solid wood. Someone, somewhere, is making an absolute fortune out of these boxes. When a box was ordered, the transport company was able to secure it on the top of a load of pallets in a vehicle already heading in the rough direction of the funeral home, and probably saved a few quid by doing that.

After an hour or so, a delivery van pulled into the

yard, carrying the part we desperately needed. Another half an hour passed and we were ready to go. I had put the test out of my mind for a while so was less nervous and some of my tension had dissipated. Once fixed, we set off to pick up the trailer, Paul apologising all the way. I did feel sorry for him, it couldn't have happened on a worse day. Both his rigid and articulated test vehicles were in very good shape and regularly maintained with no expense spared. He had pride in his 'fleet'. I wasn't remotely bothered, to be honest, I was just glad we were on the road and I would make my test on time.

We left the yard for the last time, this was 'do or die'

*For those that don't know, the 5th wheel is the horseshoe-shaped plate on the rear of the unit that the trailer pin clicks into and takes the weight of the trailer. This is the way to connect up for the test but, like everything, is different once you're out in the real world. The reason for this being that if the trailer has been dropped high (all units and axle configurations make them different heights) the unit can 'jump the pin' i.e. reverse too far back and, as has happened to people (not me I hasten to add!), the unit can back straight into the trailer headboard leaving both damaged. The method is as simple as: reversing the unit up to the trailer whilst lowering the unit suspension (done by the press of a button in the cab), backing in just far enough so the 5th wheel is underneath the trailer. Then, raise the suspension which will lift the trailer, making sure the trailer pin will locate into the 5th wheel and also lifting the trailer legs clear of the ground by a few inches, making them easier to wind up, particularly important if the trailer is loaded, plus there is less chance of damaging them when performing the 'tug check' as there is no strain on them once they are off the ground

**When releasing the trailer brake, always pause near to the button as, if you have accidently left the unit parking brake off and the whole rig starts to roll, you will be able to apply the brake with ease.   This has never happened to me, but is more common than you would think.   Drivers have been known to chase the trailer to reach the button with varying consequences including the vehicle stopping of its own accord, usually with the aid of another vehicle or building/wall, or the death of the driver as he slips over and gets crushed by his own lorry. Thankfully, these days, most units have a buzzer that will warn the driver if he opens the cab door and the parking brake is not engaged.

***There are differing methods of doing this.   I employ the '2 gentle tugs' method, which is all that is necessary for the purpose of checking.   Other drivers I have seen like to employ, what is best described as, the 'try to rip the pin off of the bottom of the trailer whilst spinning the wheels of the unit and revving the engine just to make sure it's really secured' method.   There is no need for this and it makes me wince every time I see someone doing it.   Horses for courses

****There are 5 susies consisting of;

Red airline (emergency)

This has a collar on the susie that needs to be held back while the susie is pushed into the trailer connector.

Yellow airline (service brakes)

This is the opposite of the red line, a collar on the trailer connection will need to be pushed to connect.

2 electrical connections (lights/indicators)

These simply push in, a bit like a caravan or trailer hook-up on a car, and each one has its own connection on the trailer (each one will only fit the corresponding connection, found through trial and error)

ABS line (for the trailer Anti-locking Brakes System)

The hole for this will be obvious. Simply push the plug into the connector and clip the metal securing device into place.

Make sure they are ALL connected. **ALWAYS.**

Always keep your susies clean and as straight as you can get them. Some airlines are hard to connect and the only way is to straddle them. If they are clarted in 5th wheel grease, it'll end up all over your nice clean trousers (bad) and subsequently all over your, or someone else's, cab (very bad). If one of your airlines gets kinked, it could wear out quickly or, even worse, slam the trailer brakes on whilst you are hurtling along at 56mph.

When I started writing this book, I wasn't sure whether to spell it susies or soozies or suzies. There are many ideas as to where the word comes from. Some say it's a brand name, others say it was named after the inventor (his surname was Suzenderger, apparently). Another interesting myth is that a prostitute called Susan was the first person killed by a lorry driver, strangled to death with an airline. It could possibly have been a brand name many years ago, but the other two definitions don't seem very plausible. The most believable origination of the word comes from **SUS**pended **I**nsulated **E**lectrical **L**ead**S**, so this is what I have used.   Please feel free to contact me if you have a better idea.

THE BIG ONE

Here I was, sitting in the waiting room of the Nottingham HGV test centre, doing what I thought I'd never do - waiting to take my Class 1 Large Goods Vehicle test. This is what I said I'd never do; it looked far too hard, too scary and too expensive. Why was I here, putting myself through this stress? The dream. Oh yeah, the 'dream'. I didn't want that right now, didn't care. I just wanted to get back to my nice, easy-to-drive rigid. That would do; no scary test, no reversing round corners and getting stuck. No big killing machine that could wipe out a pedestrian or the corner of a building in the blink of an eye.

To be truthful, I still couldn't reverse. I didn't know what I was doing, or how to go about it. I know this sounds weird, but my instructor had babysat me through the procedure every time, shouting louder and louder, getting more excited and animated as time wore on. I didn't have a clue. I started to seriously question whether I would know what to do, a bit late considering I'd have to prove to an examiner that I could do this, all by myself, in about 10 minutes time.

Then my name was called.

I froze for a brief moment, swallowed hard, and

followed the examiner to my vehicle, parked nice and neatly in the adjacent parking area. Another dose of stress came when parking here 20 minutes previously as my instructor, obviously feeling the pressure of all those other driving instructors watching me, nearly collapsed when I messed up the reverse into one of the spaces and had to 'take a shunt'. Christ man, get a bloody life, grow some balls, stop being so bloody anal and worrying about what a few other people think of you and your teaching skills (though, I'm sure, they were chatting amongst themselves and drinking coffee, completely oblivious, not to mention not caring less, about how my parking was going). This was it for me, I had to pass as I couldn't stand another 5 minutes of being taught by this bloke. No offence mate, but I was seriously at the end of my tether. He actually mentioned to one of his colleagues how it was one of the few jobs in which someone of his size (tiny) could belittle and shout at someone my size (approaching the proverbial brick out-house) without getting battered. Paul, you have no idea how close you came.

The next thing I knew, I was sat in the cab with my relaxed examiner, about to head off for one of the worst hours one could wish to spend whilst paying through the nose for. I did a walk round check of my vehicle followed by answering all the questions, regarding checking water and oil levels, correctly. Next, into the cones for the reversing exercise. I honestly don't remember whether the examiner was in the cab or out at this point, I think he was outside watching the cones and white lines, checking my tyres didn't run over them. I remembered talking myself through this (in my head) and being relieved once it was, thankfully successfully, over and done with. For me, this was the hardest part of the test and it was best out of the way first.

Next, we headed for the exit and, having performed the controlled stop successfully, we passed through the gates and out onto the open road. The next part of the test is a bit of a blur. I remember pulling out on the road and checking the time to see if I should be using the bus lane or not. I was immediately asked to pull up behind a parked car, leaving about a car's length in front, then being told to proceed. This is to make sure you are able to manoeuvre the lorry around an obstacle. At this point, I assumed I'd failed as I had indicated left to pull up to the kerb and left the indicator on. The examiner asked me to cancel it, which I did, but thought that was that for me. Usually, if they have to intervene, you've had it! So I figured I would complete the rest of the test as best I could as a practice for next time, when I'll have to return and do it all over again. Then it was down to the roundabout on the main road and into town, through some narrow traffic cones around roadworks, and down by the prison, where I was asked to stop, then to proceed. This was the downhill start, though the examiners never tell you it's that, they just ask you to continue to see if you're aware of it. From there, it was on to a housing estate at the top of Nottingham where I carried out the gear changing exercise. Next, we headed back down the dual carriageway to the test centre. It was all over pretty quick, yet also seemed like it had taken hours. Once at the centre, I was asked to uncouple and re-couple the trailer. I proceeded to go through everything, trailer brake on, legs down, susies uncoupled, pull the 5th wheel pin. Damn, it won't budge, try again. Nothing. Panic! I turned to my examiner and said "It won't move". I think he felt a bit sorry for me, and suggested I get into the cab and try rocking backwards and forwards (gently). This did the trick and the pin released. This was something else that I had never come across and it never crossed my instructor's mind to brief any of his pupils on it, as it had never happened before. I get the feeling that he probably did after this, though.

With the trailer hitched up again, the examiner and I sat back in the cab and he gave me my result: I PASSED!! Bloody hell, I was sweating like crazy. I thought I'd messed it up right at the start but, in hindsight, the thought that I'd failed relaxed me and I just went through the motions to finish the test. Job done, I was chuffed!

That was it, no more mirror, signal, manoeuvre! No more Paul!!! Incidentally, soon after (and on my recommendation) he joined a well-known trucking forum and used 'mirror, signal, manoeuvre' as his username, but spelled the last word wrong. He made a couple of posts until someone pulled him up on this (what with him being an instructor an' all!) and he has never been seen or heard of (online) since! His over-inflated ego wouldn't have been able to handle this simplest of mistakes and his pride wouldn't allow him to laugh over it, either.

THE ROAD AHEAD

With the excitement over, it was back to work for me the day after my test, driving my rigid, delivering steel. I spoke to the boss's son as soon as I could get hold of him on the phone and told him my good news, and asked whether they had an opening for me to drive an artic. Most companies are short of artic drivers so it shouldn't really be a problem, not forgetting that it was only a few weeks previously that the firm were willing to put me through my test and allow me to drive their trucks. It was a bit of a surprise, then, when I was told that their insurance would only cover a new driver if they had taken lessons and passed the test using the instructor that the firm used. This sounded a bit dodgy to me, but I didn't let it worry me. I later found out, as I was leaving on my very last day, that he was enraged that I didn't take my test through them and, for that reason and that reason alone, I was not allowed to drive their articulated lorries. How petty is that? I'd saved them about a grand, got qualified in a bigger, better lorry than they own, yet I wasn't allowed the chance to drive one. That obviously sealed my fate and I knew I had to find a company that would allow me to use my licence. It was their loss, they knew I was a good employee but, due to petty jealousy, they would eventually be losing me. First though, the rent still needed to be paid…..

This job took me all over the UK and wasn't too bad when you were out on the open road. I did manage to get a few Scotland runs, but mainly seemed to end up in the Manchester or Liverpool areas. It was handy, at times, having a HIAB crane on my vehicle, as I could just unload myself and not have to wait for a crane or JCB to do it. On occasions though, I couldn't be bothered so would say the HIAB was not working, knowing full well that the building site had a perfectly good machine that would unload me a lot quicker than I could do it myself.

The problem was with weight. I mainly delivered steel re-bar (reinforcement bar) and steel mesh. The mesh was loaded in the yard by an overhead crane, and could weigh three of four tonnes in one lift. The sheets were all bound together with steel so hard to separate. My HIAB could only lift a couple of tons at a time and, on more than a few occasions, I lifted a lot more on that crane than was permissible. If you did it right, you could just about lift the mesh off the lorry bed. It would sag in the middle but could be moved side to side, just about. When the crane was at its shortest was when it could lift the most weight so, the higher you lifted, or the further you swung the load round to the side, the less it would be able to carry. This was not good as, when the weight was too much, the HIAB would simply just drop down. You could be swinging the mesh over to the side of the truck, dragging it along the lorry bed, when it would just drop and refuse to lift again. All you could do was push the mesh with the crane and watch it come crashing down on the ground, hopefully not puncturing a tyre in the process.

One day, I had been given 5 drops around Manchester, Leeds and Sheffield. I had delivered Manchester and Leeds with no problems and was heading south on the M1 to my final drop. It was coming up to 5 o'clock so I phoned the office to see if the site would still be open in about half an hour, as most sites shut at 5pm. They called back a few minutes later saying the site would be open and just to unload with the HIAB. This was common practice as some sites didn't have security fences or gates. I found the site, a new road of houses, but there was security fencing all round and the gate was locked. I drove round the whole perimeter but no-one was around, so I headed back to the yard to finish for the day.

The next morning, I got my paperwork and found I had deliveries in Manchester, Leeds and Doncaster. No problem, I would just load the new drops on top of the old, and finish up in Sheffield again. The day didn't go well. I managed to get stuck in traffic on the M62 and held up at a couple of drops waiting for other lorries to leave the site or waiting to get unloaded by the tower crane. I was on the M1 south again, around the same place, when I phoned the office asking what to do with the Sheffield drop. The boss's son answered and I explained that the site had been shut yesterday at the same time and, as today was Friday, it was less likely it would be open. He replied with "Erm, just head over and try to deliver it, someone might be there". Ok, whatever you say. I headed straight for Tibshelf services, waited for 20 minutes, before heading back to the yard and parking up. It was now well past 5pm so I knew the office staff would be gone for the weekend. The following Monday, I explained that the yard was shut. Thankfully, they took the delivery off me and gave it to someone else to deliver first thing that morning. What a waste of time, not to mention fuel, that would have been. If the site was shut at 5.30pm on a Thursday, it would be shut at the same time on a Friday, no question. If the boss's son had phoned the site, and someone was willing to await my delivery, I would have gone. I was not prepared to go on his whim though, not on a Friday at rush hour!

Thankfully, these were the days when the only 'spy in the cab' was a tachograph. Some large companies had just started using GPS trackers fitted in the cab and, with the press of a button, they could look at a computer screen and see exactly where the truck was, where it had been, and what it had been doing for the past 24 hours. I could not have got away with the above trick with one of those fitted! I have only driven one truck with a tracker fitted and, for most of the time, it didn't affect me. I was driving a green and white liveried Scania for a (very) well-known company and was doing a regular run carrying biomass in a walking floor trailer. The power station I regularly delivered to could be accessed two different ways. One way was over the hills, but shorter and the other was about 5 miles longer, but the roads straighter and with less hills. Time wise, the shorter road was about 5 minutes quicker, but would use more fuel. I used to get bored going one way all the time as I was making three or four round trips every day, so would break up the monotony by using the other route. One morning, I had already made a delivery to the power station and been back to the yard to reload for load number two. I had been the longer way for the first run, so decided to go the shorter route for the second. There was also another reason for this: It was winter and the longer route was a busier road so, first thing in the morning, the road had been gritted and well used so clear of any ice. By the time I had made a round trip, the road over the hills had chance to be gritted (it was a worse road for ice and snow due to its elevation and location) so that was now safe to use. I had turned off the main road and had been on the alternative route for about 5 minutes when my phone rang. I answered (it was a hands free cab phone) and Alex in the office said "Was the road closed with roadworks or an accident when you set off this morning?"

"No" I replied, "Why?"

He came back with "Well, you're going a different way now to what you did earlier, why is that?"

I just told him that there wasn't really much in it and the other road, though longer, was safer first thing in the morning. He also queried why I hadn't phoned in that morning as I had been held up at the power station for half an hour. I was waiting for another of our trucks to unload, it's the only place I am delivering to, so what difference would it make?

It just goes to show that you never know who's watching you. Creepy.

Working the HIAB was easy once you got used to it, and we got an extra £20 per day in our wages if we used it. This was regardless of whether you used it once or 10 times. Still, it all helped. There were occasions when you didn't need to use it as the site had a crane, but everyone would still claim for it. The hardest part was getting onto the back of the truck and chaining up the load. We loaded our own vehicles at the steelworks, and would use lumps of wood under each lift, so the chains could easily pass underneath. This was easy when loading directly onto the flat bed but a lot harder when loading on top of mesh or other lengths of bar. For a start, nothing was flat, and it could be an onerous task trying to load some of the strange shaped bar, trying to get it to interlock with each other so it could be lifted off again, and so it didn't overhang the sides of the vehicle. Not easy when the loader is impatient and waiting to load 3 other trucks after yours. This task was even worse when loading on to mesh as it was hard to walk on. I have size 12 feet which made it slightly easier as most mesh was made up of 10 inch squares. Some square gaps were a lot bigger and I have fallen over on many occasions with my foot down the hole and my leg bent at a strange angle as I lay on the load! I have many scars on my arms and legs from this job from various scrapes. It's a wonder I never got tetanus, or worse, as the steel was always rusty and I never had time to clean up after. Another crap part of the job when delivering to building sites is that, in the winter it's muddy and in summer it's dusty so it was almost impossible to keep the inside of your cab clean. Some drivers changed their shoes before they got in their truck, but this didn't seem to make much difference. In the sweltering heat of summer, you may have had to wait for an hour or two to unload and, unless you were willing to sit with the window closed, dust would sail in through the opening. AACHOOO!!!

My worst accident and injury, whilst working for this firm, was my own fault, completely and utterly! I'd love to say it wasn't and blame them, but I can't.

Another driver and I were waiting to load at the yard. We had started at 6am and the time was nearly 11 by now. One of the large overhead cranes had broken down and, though it was now fixed, there were urgent loads that needed to be away and delivered before ours were. We decided that we would head up to a nearby layby on the A38 to get a cup of tea from the regular caravan that was parked there. We climbed up the steep bank at the side of the yard and crossed the busy road to the layby. I ordered a cup of tea and a fried egg sandwich. After about 5 minutes our food was ready and we headed back down to the steelworks. The slope was very steep and about 30ft high. I had got about a quarter of the way down when I slipped and tumbled right to the bottom. The other driver managed to arrive at the bottom safely and, laughing, asked if I was alright. I said I was, but my leg hurt. I also announced how proud I was that I didn't spill my tea or drop my sandwich. I started to feel a bit sick. My right leg had bent, the foot and calf folding up underneath me as I fell, so I had effectively 'ridden' my leg all the way down. No wonder it hurt. I decided nothing was broken and stood up to walk it off. Walking it off is one of those things that men always seem to do and, in the most part, works but, on this occasion, it didn't and made me feel dizzy, not to mention in agony, so I sat down for a while and ate, which didn't really help except to make me feel even more sick.

About 10 minutes later, I stood up and, deciding that my leg was getting better, headed over to my lorry. By now, it was time to load and, very kindly (and to make up for his amusement at my predicament) the other driver jumped on the back of my wagon and loaded it for me. I wouldn't have managed. He loaded me with 3 drops in Manchester so at least I was in for an easy day.

I arrived in Manchester hoping that the rest on the journey would have helped my leg heal. Wrong! It had now stiffened up and I could barely move it. I hobbled out of the cab, cursing the high cab of the Mercedes Actros, and unsecured the ratchet straps holding the load. A forklift lifted off two stacks of re-bar so I didn't have to use the HIAB, thankfully.

On arrival at my second drop, I noted that the address was the same for the third drop too. Even better. The building site foreman came over and said the re-bar would be forklifted off a few yards down the road and stored in the warehouse, the mesh would be needed in the site behind me.

The re-bar was unloaded and stashed away in no time and I reversed back through the gates of the site. I then hobbled out of the cab again to unload the re-bar. Where I was parked on site was only about the width of the gates so, not only did I have to hobble very carefully on uneven ground, I also had to squeeze my way round the vehicle whilst not being able to see where I was going (or what I was standing on).

Finally, I was empty and heading back to Mansfield. I arrived at the yard and parked up. I usually, at this point, would take my bag (complete with sleeping bag and maps) to my car, before heading up the outer stairs to leave my signed delivery paperwork in a cubby hole outside the office which would normally take 2 minutes. On this occasion it took about half an hour. I was shuffling at this stage, my leg being extremely painful to walk on. I somehow managed to drive home and that's where I stayed for the rest of the week, unpaid. I never did go to the doctor but, on closer inspection, my ankle was twisted, my knee was damaged, and my calf muscle was very painful right up the middle.

I am a believer in karma, 'what goes around comes around' or whatever you want to call it so the above incident may possibly be linked to the one below, which happened a few months previously......

Much the same as the last story, I had started at 6am, hoping to get loaded in good time and away. Nope, there was a problem with the machinery in the steelworks so they couldn't cut the steel to the correct lengths we needed, not to mention a huge backlog of trucks that needed to be loaded. I knew this would be a long day. Lunchtime came and went, still nothing, and I was getting very bored. Another problem was that I had arranged to be off the next day. Now, I am not really one for chucking a 'sicky' but, if the occasion calls for it (i.e. I need a day off for something important but at very short notice), I'll take one. This company were not the best at accommodating their drivers' needs, as is mentioned further on in this book, so I didn't feel remotely bad. I should also point out that they don't pay any sick pay either, so it's no real loss to them. I could see where this day was going though, they'd expect me to still leave here at 2pm, be in Manchester for 4pm, hopefully getting both deliveries done. The reality is though that both sites shut at 5pm (I knew this as I had delivered to both previously) so I would possibly get one load delivered, then have to park at a service station for the night, and deliver the second load the next morning. Bang goes my day off!

I was called in to load at 1.45pm, which was looking good. If I could get them to load slowly enough, it wouldn't be worth me leaving today. It was 2.45 by the time I was loaded and strapped down. I phoned the office and luckily the boss's son didn't answer as he would have been awkward and told me to go regardless. I explained that there was little point me leaving today as I doubt I would get any of my drops done and "Would I not be better off just leaving in the morning with them…?" After a pause, the reply came back in the affirmative. Result! An early finish and my day off in the morning. Not without its consequence though, it would seem…!

Fortunately, as well as not dropping my sandwich or spilling my tea when I took a tumble, I never dropped anything off of the back of my lorry either*. We did have to load some awkward shapes of steel bar, some of it being difficult to strap down. I know of one driver that had been loaded with a large bag (similar to a cement bag that a builder's merchant uses) containing small, angled, pieces of steel. Instead of tying the handles of the bag together and strapping it down tightly, he decided to just sling it up in the middle of his load, hoping it would be held in by the bar either side. It was, but the small pieces of steel worked their way out of the bag and under the bar, dropping onto the road all along the motorway between Mansfield and Leeds. They were small but would still do a lot of damage to a tyre or windscreen. Another driver loaded his trailer with coiled steel reels, weighing about 2 tonnes each, from a steelworks in Wales. He had strapped them down, but not well enough and, as he pulled away from a set of traffic lights, the rear one rolled off straight onto the bonnet of a BMW, crushing it. Thankfully, nobody was injured.

By now, I was ferociously looking for another job, I would have done anyway regardless as to whether I had passed my Class 1 test or not, as a few incidents over the last few months had made me start to dislike working there. Firstly, I was sent out in a lorry with no working night heater, in the middle of a very cold winter, and told that I 'must' stay out for the night instead of coming back to base (which was only 20 miles away from where I parked for the night) or else the company would deduct the fuel costs from my wages. I'm no mug, and knew it was illegal, but it adds to the bad feeling of working somewhere under those circumstances.

On another occasion, I had started at 6 in the morning, delivered 5 drops around Manchester and headed back to the yard. I was just finishing at 5pm when the boss's son (him again) came down and told me I had to go round to a warehouse a mile down the road to help them move some steel sheets. Normally, this wouldn't have been an issue as it was easy enough (reverse the lorry in, crane on steel, pull outside, wait, reverse back in, unload) and usually only took an hour. On this occasion, I had asked if I could finish at a reasonable time as my daughter had a concert at her school and I always thought it very important that I should attend any event like this. When I protested, I was threatened with the sack and told that I had a problem with authority. I don't, but I do have a problem with an abuse of authority and petty arseholes. I did the job, and still managed to make it home in time, but hated the place (and more so him) after that.

The best one, from my point of view, was when I had to deliver a mobile phone mast to a site just outside Liverpool. My lorry wasn't equipped to carry this, as it required a 'goal post' style bracket (which actually resembled an 'H' shaped rugby goal post) to hold the mast high enough above the cab. Then, at the rear of the bed, a smaller, lower bracket was needed to secure the back of the mast to and hold it up so the angle wasn't too steep. When I arrived at work on this particular morning, I could see the new posts welded on to the bulkhead and the garage looked like they had made a good job of it. The firm had their own garage onsite complete with inspection pits and good mechanics. The boss of this little empire was the boss's wife's brother, a ghastly little man that no-one appeared to like. All the other lads were fine though, and couldn't be more helpful. Attached to the bed of my wagon (with a ratchet strap) was a flimsy bracket, sitting about a foot high, made of thin steel, and measuring about a foot in width. This looked ridiculous, not to mention dangerous, so I refused to load a 5 foot diameter mast onto this bracket. The garage boss came in to the canteen, where I was waiting with a cup of coffee, and told me there was nothing wrong with this bracket, it was perfectly good for the job, and I should go and load up the mast (which was waiting about 3 miles down the road), strap it down and drive it back to the garage to let them judge for themselves as to whether it was safe or not. I told him that, as I wasn't happy with the bracket, that I would not be loading the mast on to it and driving it on a public highway. The garage boss was walking away at this point and, obviously not being used to being told 'no', stopped in his tracks, spun round and repeated (louder this time) that I should load the mast, strap it down and drive it back to the garage so they could judge for themselves. I told him a firm 'no' again. With this he stormed out. A few minutes later, the senior driver arrived for work. He had worked here for about 30 years and had respect from everyone, including the management. I told him the problem and he took one look at the bracket and immediately said "There is no way you are loading a mast on to that flimsy piece of crap". I waited for an hour or so until the garage made me a much sturdier bracket and headed off to load the mast. A good lesson for everyone is to never be bullied into taking something or loading something you are not happy with, regardless of who says 'it'll be ok'. It's your licence and your vehicle. You are in charge and you make the decisions.

*Once loaded, I would strap my load up tightly. Then I would leave the yard and pull over on the motorway slip road (in the hard shoulder, out of the way) and check the straps were still tight. A load will often come loose once it has settled and this is a good habit to get into.

A WASTE OF TIME

Since passing my test, I had been scouring the local job paper for adverts so I could put my newly-learned skills to the test. One particular advert, from a frozen food delivery company based in Newark, caught my eye. I liked the idea of working for this company as they had a fleet of new trucks and had depots across the UK. I spoke to the Transport Manager over the phone, explaining that I had only just passed my test, and he seemed pretty keen and invited me in for an interview and test drive.

The big day arrived and, having booked a day off of work and being suitably, smartly, attired for the occasion, I set off for Newark. As soon as I sat down in the TM's office, he told me that they would not be able to offer me a job as I didn't have the relevant experience they always require, which is 2 years. I was astounded! Why tell me over the phone that I could come for an interview and that my lack of experience "Wouldn't be a problem"? I assumed there was little chance of getting the job, but figured I would at least get a test drive in one of their vehicles so the day wouldn't be a complete write-off. He said that it wasn't worth doing this as I had no hope of getting a job. What a waste of a day's holiday, travel costs and travel time to and from Newark, and bothering to get dressed up. All for nothing.

A STRANGE COINCIDENCE

I happened to stop in at Lymm Truckstop late one afternoon, having delivered my load of steel to a couple of sites near Liverpool and Chester. I was wandering round the shop looking at the array of 'bling' available for trucks, not to mention the price tags that went with them when, from behind me, a voice I recognised said "Hello there". I turned round and saw it was Eddie. Eddie had, until recently, driven for the same firm I was working for and, having fallen out with the boss's son, had managed to find himself another job. I had heard that he was on container work, driving a Renault Magnum. I liked the idea of driving one of these as they are one of the highest cabs available, and they look different too. They are unpopular with a lot of hauliers as they are heavy, so obviously the amount of load you can carry will be less. The reason for this is the 'walk-through' cab which, unlike other lorry cabs, has no engine 'hump' so the floor is completely flat. To be this high, there is a lot of extra weight involved, obviously. I chatted with Eddie for a while and told him the problem I was having finding a job driving an artic. He said that his boss was looking for a driver and he would pass on my phone number and give me a good reference. I assumed he would probably forget and this would be the last I heard of it. We said our goodbyes, I was heading back to

Nottingham to go home and he was heading for the shower as he was parking up for the night. I gave his Magnum a quick glance-over as I headed back across the truck park to where my own wagon was parked. These cabs seemed like they belonged to a train, having steps to one side of the door. The windscreen was huge, and I imagined myself piloting this huge beast, high above everything else on the road.

Later that night, once I was home, my phone rang. It was Eddie, just letting me know that he had passed my number onto his boss. The firm had 4 lorries, all Renault Magnums, 2 on container work and 2 on fridge work (with one of those occasionally going to Europe). The driver on the Euro run was leaving so Eddie thought it might be possible for me to take over his truck on container work, the boss having decided that he would be stopping Euro work altogether. Things were looking up. Later that week, I received a call from the boss. We had a good chat about driving and what the work would entail. If I wanted the job, I could start the following week. I would be running containers out of Felixstowe docks for delivery anywhere in the UK. This sounded great! The only problem was that my truck would not be available as the driver, who was supposed to be leaving the next week, had decided that he was entitled to give a months' notice so would be staying on for a couple more weeks. It was decided that I would be working with Eddie for the first 2 weeks until my truck became available and this suited me as, although I don't really like working with other people, it would be very handy to learn the ins and outs of the docks from someone that had done the job. It was time to hand my notice in to the boss's son......

THE LAST WORD

I already had a couple of days holiday booked for later in the week, so I would give a week's notice on the Friday when I was off. Previous to this, I had another run-in with the boss's son. We generally loaded our own trucks with steel, as mentioned previously, acting as a 'slinger'. Having reversed into the steelworks, the steel would be lifted over using an overhead crane and the driver (in other words, me) would be on the back of the truck to guide it into position and undo the chains. On this occasion, I was nearly knocked off the vehicle as the young lad operating the crane was not paying attention and actually talking to one of his workmates, instead of watching what he was doing. There was no point shouting as no-one would hear you over the din of the place. I immediately jumped off the lorry and refused, point blank, to continue loading. I was not a trained slinger so would not be doing this again. There was a massive 'hoo-har', and a bigger deal made of this than seemed necessary and one worker, the useless lad's uncle, got quite angry with me on a couple of occasions after I refused to get on the lorry. He would storm off to the office in a rage. After a phone call, down came the boss's son to sort me out, no doubt. I will always remember the look on his face when I point blank refused to load the vehicle as it was not safe and I was not trained for the job and even better to see him, complete with nice white shirt and shiny shoes, climbing onto the truck and loading it for me. He must have hated me (more-so than he already did). He said that he was booked in for a Banksmen's course at the end of the week, which would allow him to show me (and all the other drivers) how to load a vehicle safely thus we would be qualified in future. No excuses not to get on with it after that, then. Fair enough.

Unfortunately for him, I was the only driver kicking up a stink about this. Trailers would be loaded overnight, so the artic drivers just had to pick up a trailer in the morning. The other rigid drivers weren't making a fuss about loading, so it was all for me, though one rigid driver did start refusing to load his vehicle in solidarity with me, but relented when I told him I had handed my notice in and didn't care anymore.

It was Friday, I was off work on my day off, when I phoned the office to tell them I was handing in my weeks' notice. I asked to speak to the boss's son and was told that I couldn't as he was away all day on a Banksmen's course. This felt like a nice victory for me. Petty? Yes! Silly? Maybe. Justified? Absolutely, as it is what the firm should have been doing anyway to help make it safer for drivers loading their own vehicles. If I had fallen off and broken my leg (or worse), who would have been responsible? The steel works? No, not their problem, they just crane the steel to the lorry and the driver does the rest.   The haulage firm?   Nope, not their problem either, they would probably turn round and claim the driver shouldn't have been loading his own lorry.   Now that an issue had been raised and the boss's son had taken this course, it would be easier for the firm to be held to account for any accidents that occur as they have admitted liability by training drivers to do this part of the job.   What a way to leave, though!

THE BIG DAY
IN THE BIG VEHICLE

This was it! The day had arrived. I was to meet Eddie on a local industrial estate, where he kept his lorry. I was both excited and nervous as I would have to drive with an experienced driver in the cab with me, which could be good or bad. Any mistakes would be noticed, there would be no hiding them. On the other hand, he would be on hand to help me out if I messed up completely so I was glad he was there. We set off for Felixstowe heading first to the A1, then onto the A14 and I soon got the feel for the Magnum, and thoroughly enjoyed the run to the docks.

Once we arrived at Felixstowe, we fuelled up, and headed off to get our paperwork from the company we were carrying for. Out of office hours, the paperwork was left in a cabinet for us. This paperwork told us which number our container was, and which area we would collect it from and where it was to be delivered. Within Felixstowe there a 2 main dock areas, Landguard and Trinity. Landguard was usually quieter so Eddie was glad that we were heading here on this morning. We pulled up at the security office and took the paperwork in, and they gave us a printout detailing which 'lane' and which number 'pad' we were to proceed to. Once there, it was a case of waiting for a RTG (Rubber Tyre Gripper) to make its way to us and load our container, which was located somewhere in the stack to our left. This can take anything from 2 minutes, to several hours and priority is given to the loading and unloading of boats, so drivers just have to wait. Every container has a unique number and, once it's unloaded from the ship, is placed on a stack ready for collection, with the information stored on computer.

Once the container has been loaded onto your trailer, or 'Skelly' (skeletal) as they are called, it's a simple case of closing the twist locks (by twisting them into the 'lock' position, amazingly) and driving back to the security gate where a guard will check the paperwork and security number against the security lock on the container*.

All container deliveries are timed, meaning they are booked in for unload at a specific time. Most places are flexible so you can arrive early, but it's best not to be late. Also, a driver should never enter a container to unload, or help unload, it. Apparently, as the container belongs to a shipping company, we are not insured in case of accident, so all unloading is left to the person that receives the delivery. This means that, once the driving is over and the box is safely delivered to the customer, a container driver has only to sit in his cab and wait. They do say that container drivers have the cleanest cabs, due to the spare time involved. The customer has 3 hours to empty a 20ft container, and 4 hours for a 40ft and this goes for loading as well as emptying. Sometimes, these time limits are exceeded and the company will get charged waiting time, or Demurrage.

Our box was for delivery to the New Spitalfields Market (thankfully located on the outskirts of London instead of down some tiny, very busy, side street) so, with the sat-nav set, we headed west along the A14 and south onto the A12. On arrival at the market we were glad to see it wasn't too busy and parked so we could find our delivery point and opened the container doors. I was told to always stand clear as you never know how well the container has been loaded. Some boxes are crammed so full that the goods push the doors and fall out, causing injury to the unsuspecting driver below. Fortunately, our load was potatoes from Cyprus and was loaded well on pallets. We found where to unload and the stall owner borrowed a forklift truck. His mate jumped into the container and, once a pallet truck was lifted into the back, proceeded to unload the tatties. The guy in the container was quite small and was struggling to turn the pallets and move them to the back of the truck so the forklift could reach them as they were loaded high, so Eddie hopped up into the back to help out, even though he shouldn't have done, but sometimes the job doesn't work that way. Unloading was quick and, for helping him out, the market stall owner gave Eddie a (huge) bag of the

Cypriot potatoes we had just delivered. Eddie was, for some reason, not too fussed about this and, when we arrived home, gave me the whole big bag minus a few he took for his dinner that night. They were some of the best potatoes I have ever tasted and had a lovely red skin on them. Mashed, chipped, boiled or roasted, they tasted great! I know it's only a bag of spuds, but it's nice to get something free during the course of a working day.

The first week went without incident and the pair of us delivered a load a day, as was Eddie's mantra, "One box a day, no more", but things didn't always work out like this as we'll find out later.

I was supposed to be with Eddie for two weeks but he decided that, whilst I was there to drive his truck, it would be a good time for him to take a week's holiday. I found out about this on the Thursday and worried about going it alone for the next three days. Still, I knew my way round the docks, and the truck, so things could have been worse and, in truth, I was looking forward to getting out on the open road by myself.

*If you are new to container work, or fancy giving it a go, be aware of these points;

-This is very important. ALWAYS check and DOUBLE CHECK that your twist locks are undone or open when you're waiting to get a container lifted off. The RTGs are huge, the driver is very high up and you are probably like an ant to him, the tyres are higher than your lorry cab so he won't feel a thing if he runs over your foot. Or head. The safest place to sit is in your cab but if your twist locks are still closed, the container will start to lift, and the whole lorry will go with it. This has happened on too many occasions and resulted in the death of the driver as the whole rig comes crashing back down to earth and, with the weight of the cab forcing it to hang down, guess which part hits the deck first?

- Always park within the marked bay or pad, and make sure that all wheels are within the marked lines, and the lorry is as straight as possible, as the RTG driver uses these lines for guidance. I parked slightly wonky once at Seaforth and the tyre from an RTG almost hit my truck. Never again, I made sure the lorry was dead straight after this.

-When loading at the docks, always check that the container is placed the correct way round on your lorry, with the doors to the back. It may sound odd, but the crane drivers do sometimes get it wrong. If you don't notice, you'll get to your delivery point (which could be 400 miles away) and won't be able to unload!

-Always check that the container is located on all 4 pins. Sometimes, it can look like it is in position but, when you come to close the twist locks, one or two of the pins aren't located in the container. A simple remedy to this is drive forward fast and slam on the brakes. That usually does it. If not? Repeat.

-Always stand clear when opening the doors as some containers are jam-packed so that the goods inside can come tumbling out and, if you're not careful, cause damage or injury.

-Always check the manifest to see what you are carrying. Some containers can carry liquid (and not just the ISO containers). If you don't check the paperwork, you'll find out when you first brake sharply. The liquid will push to the front, surge backwards, then crash to the front again, which is when it'll push the truck forward. If you're not ready for it, you could end up smashing into the vehicle in front. Failing that, you may well tip over on the next roundabout due to the water surging sideways. Many loads will be expensive, so you'll want to know whether you should park somewhere safe for the night. On a couple of occasions, I would be told to make sure I parked in our secure yard (which we didn't have) as I was carrying £80k of booze on board. It goes without saying to never tell anyone where you are going or what you are carrying. If in doubt, just say you're carrying recycled newspaper.

-Never load above the height of an open top container. An open top is exactly that: a container with no roof, though most do have a sheet that will be secured over the top to keep the load dry. I have seen a few trucks on the road with bits sticking out the top, and have had crane drivers trying to leave the load protruding by four or five feet. Obviously, the sheet won't be able to fit on over the load but, more importantly, these containers are still stackable, both in the container storage area and on the ship, so anything over the height will cause problems (and possibly a return trip back to get it reloaded, which your boss will have to pay for)

-Always remove your container lock! Your company should issue you with a large container lock that fits round the bars on both back doors for when you leave the vehicle unattended, or sleep for the night in a layby. It's easy to remember to put the lock on, but can be hard to remember to remove it. I have known people, though have never done it myself, who have left the lock on and only realised when they watch the container being lifted off at the docks, when it's too late. If you can't get the crane drivers' attention, a poor truck driver in America or Japan will not be able to open the container when they deliver it. I wouldn't like this to happen to me as it could take ages to find someone to get the thing off. My trick? Always leave the keys to the lock on your dashboard so you see them before driving off the next morning. If you remove the lock straight away, you won't have the problem of explaining to your boss where his £50 lock has gone.

GOING ALONE

Monday couldn't come soon enough. I was raring to go. I was slightly nervous, admittedly, but that feeling was over-ruled by the excitement of finally being a proper trucker. Eddie's new Magnum had a sat-nav fitted so finding places shouldn't be a problem. I took my night-out gear with me (Eddie and I never had a night out in the first week, though it came close when we were supposed to have a run to Scotland but it thankfully got cancelled at the last minute), took plenty of provisions (the cab also had a fridge under the bunk) and my trusty portable DVD player which Eddie had commandeered in the first week and watched a good selection of war and action films whilst sat in the passenger seat.

At 6am on the Monday morning I was heading south towards Felixstowe, alone. On arriving at the office, I collected my paperwork and found I would be loading with an empty container for a waste paper recyclers in Erith, near Dartford. That sounded easy enough. Another Renault Magnum pulled in next to me and the driver jumped out for a chat. He asked where I was heading for and, on finding out that I was off to Erith, he started giving me some directions. Erith is easy enough to find, head over the Dartford Crossing and follow the signs. On the road to Erith, the recyclers would be sign posted on the right, just before the roundabout. He then told me that the access road had a 10 foot low bridge height marker but, due to the bridge now having been raised (actually, the road had been dug out and lowered) I would be ok to go under it with my 14 foot high container. Hmm, was he winding me up? Should I believe him? I did think it would be a pretty mean trick and he seemed genuine enough, best to be careful though.

I set the sat-nav for Erith. I say 'set', it was one of those deals where you had to phone the sat-nav supplier and give them the postcode and/or road name of your destination and they would then remotely set it up for you. This worked well, my only problem being that I find it hard to come up with the correct word for the corresponding letter in the Phonetic Alphabet and usually end up with the first word springing to mind being a rude one so, instead of 'Bravo', I'd think 'bollocks', Alpha/arse, Foxtrot....well, you get the picture. It was always best for me to write down the letter and corresponding word before phoning to save any embarrassment at a later stage.

The sat-nav guided me west on the A14 then south on the A12, M25 to the Dartford Crossing and westbound to Erith. I was always impressed how this tiny box sat on the dashboard could actually tell what lane I was in on a dual carriageway and would tell me to get into the correct lane long before a junction.

Just before reaching Erith, sure enough, I saw the sign for the waste centre and the low bridge warning triangle. Despite what the friendly trucker had told me, and the soothing voice of the sat-nav narrator telling me to turn right, I couldn't bring myself to do it. I kept straight on to see if there was another way round. I went all the way round the roundabout, heading back in the direction I had just come from. Nope, no other roads or signs. Damn! I turned round again and, this time, braved the right turn to the low bridge. To my relief, the road beneath the bridge had been lowered and I sailed under. This was actually quite a tight bridge due to the road lowering as, I assume, the added concrete was to strengthen the bridge and, in the process, made the entrance a lot narrower. I turned left into the yard and onto the left one of two weighbridges. I went into the small office, handed over my paperwork, and the man told me that I had to reverse on to one of the bays just back a bit in the direction I had just entered. There were two ways to do this: either reverse back off the weighbridge or go forwards, round to the right, right again, and back in the entrance. There were no other lorries around and I figured I might lose my bay (and end up waiting for ages for another truck to load if someone else got there first) so decided reversing back would be easier. It turned out that it wasn't.

The diagram below explains better, but the left weighbridge was offset to the left so, when entering, you would drive past the office wall and the left weighbridge was about 2 foot further to the left of, and beyond, this. Not much, is it? I started to reverse off the weighbridge, watching my tyres as the sides were raised metal which would cut the tyres nicely if touched. I then started to kink the trailer a small amount to the right so it would clear the office wall. I maybe kinked it slightly too far and needed to correct it. I obviously couldn't move the unit too far left or right due to the metal waiting to eat my tyres, so kept reversing back. I then shunted forward, then back again. I am sweating writing this as the fear is starting to well up inside me again. This is the exact reason why I NEVER wanted to drive big bendy trucks. I continued reversing and the trailer was now heading too far over to the right towards a fence but my unit had just cleared the weighbridge so I should be able to swing it round and bring the trailer over to the left. Which I did. Badly. The trailer was now at a 45 degree angle to the unit, heading towards the weighbridge office wall. I pulled forward, I pulled backwards, all the while trying to manoeuvre the cab so the trailer straightens up. Not a chance. It's worth remembering here that all new articulated lorry drivers think they should make massive swinging movements with the steering wheel to get the trailer where they want it to go. The reality is that you end up over-steering and making a complete dog's dinner of it all. Nice gentle movements and don't panic. It's easy to say now, but I was starting to really panic. I couldn't move forwards without hitting the weighbridge, I couldn't straighten up as the office wall was getting closer. I could also see two lorries waiting in line behind me to get on the weighbridge and, to top it all off, a small crowd of office workers had now gathered in the windows to my right and were watching me struggling away, no doubt having a good laugh and wondering why this man didn't just reverse straight, and what were all those dark patches appearing on his t-shirt?

I was stuck. Well and truly………

Weighbridge diagram

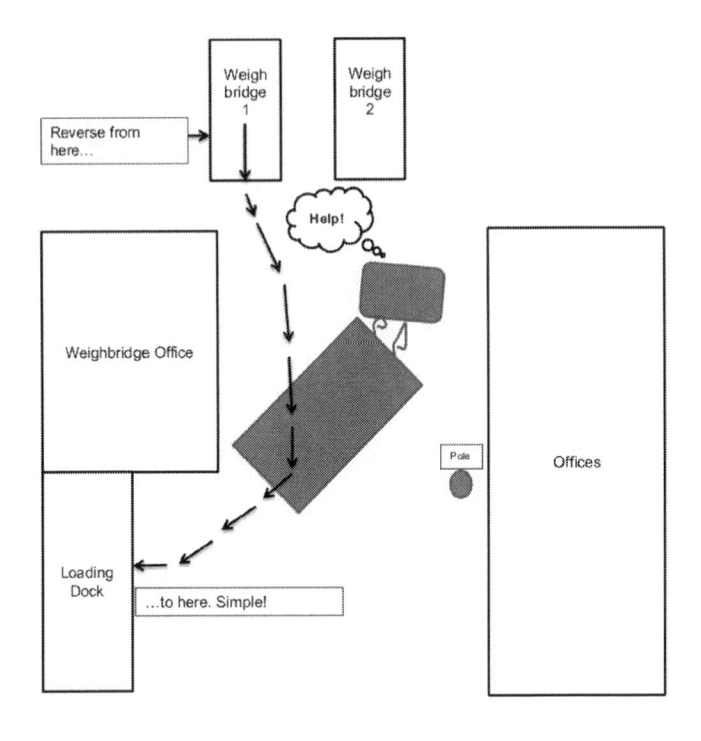

```
                          ┌──────┐  ┌──────┐
                          │Weigh │  │Weigh │
                          │bridge│  │bridge│
                          │  1   │  │  2   │
┌──────────────┐          └──────┘  └──────┘
│ Reverse from │→
│ here...      │
└──────────────┘
                                 (Help!)
┌─────────────────┐
│                 │
│                 │
│ Weighbridge     │
│ Office          │                    ┌──────┐
│                 │                    │ Pole │     ┌─────────┐
│                 │                    └──────┘     │ Offices │
│                 │                                 │         │
│   ┌──────┐     │                                 │         │
│   │Loading│    │                                 │         │
│   │Dock   │ ┌──────────────────┐                 │         │
└───┴──────┴───┤ ...to here. Simple! │              └─────────┘
              └──────────────────┘
```

After what seemed like an age, but was probably only a couple of minutes, one of the truckers waiting in line behind me came up and started giving me directions and motions of which way to turn the wheel etc. Within a few shunts backwards and forwards, I was heading back in a straight line towards my goal. All that remained was a blindside reverse onto one of the bays and I was finished. The bays were wide and, due to some idiot blocking the weighbridge for the last 20 minutes, no other trucks were able to get in so I had no problem lining up and reversing round (though I do seem to remember I took a few shunts and jumped out to look twice as there was a telegraph pole right in the way of where I needed to swing the cab round).

Once on the bay, I was quickly loaded, weighed out and back on the road, this time opting to go straight ahead out of the yard.

Different yards have different methods for unloading or loading containers. Some have proper marked bays, some have a forklift and a man with a pallet truck, and some are unloaded (but very rarely loaded) by hand. One particular yard I heard about had a good way of loading scrap metal for shipment to China – they would lift the container off the lorry, tip it up and move it against a platform where, above, a machine would push the scrap over the edge into the box. It was then turned back the correct way round and placed on the lorry. One yard I delivered to on my second day had a fixed loading ramp that I had to reverse up against. This seemed easy enough, the yard was huge with nothing in it so there was plenty of room for error. I reversed back and thought I was lined up nicely (from the cab, you couldn't actually see the metal midsection of the ramp, just the outer concrete ramp). The lad that was guiding me back whistled for me to stop, go forwards, and try again. I did. He whistled again, this time coming to the cab window to tell me I was 3 inches too far to the side. 3 inches? That's pretty good isn't it? Close enough, surely?   Nope, the middle ramp flap that is positioned in the entrance of the container has an inch of space either side. Who built this thing? It's hard enough getting a trailer somewhere in the ball park of a loading ramp, let alone with an inch tolerance either side. Still, I located it correctly on the third go and decided it was possible in the end.

The following week, Eddie was back at work, fresh from his weeks' holiday. This meant I would now get my own lorry. It was an older Renault Magnum with no fridge or sat-nav, but it was mine. I collected it over the weekend, fuelled it up and took it home for a wash and filled it with my maps, night out gear and tins of food. It wasn't perfect but, as I said, it was mine. I no longer had to worry about leaving my maps under the bunk, or leaving my night out gear stowed away as no one else would be driving it. When I was driving the rigid on the steel job, it was my regular truck, but the night man would occasionally use it so I would take my bedding, maps, anything that was mine really, out every night, which was a right pain. I had my brand new Nottingham A to Z stolen on my first day, so learnt the lesson the hard way. It could have been worse; another driver left his night out gear in his cab, as most do, and the night man actually slept in his sleeping bag. As if that wasn't bad enough, the night man had some sort of skin problem that caused him to come out in a rash and the dead skin would flake off so you can imagine the state of the inside of the poor guy's bed. I think he said he burnt it after that.

So, having my own private space was important, especially as things were about to change and I would be spending even more time in my cab.

We were used to working out of Felixstowe but our boss had decided this wasn't paying so we stopped working for the transport company in Felixstowe and started up with another, based in a container transshipment yard near Gorton in Greater Manchester. We would occasionally be loading or unloading here but would mainly be working out of Seaforth Docks near Liverpool.

Eddie had been to Seaforth once before and said it was a nightmare, always a long queue, a pain to get to, and generally wasn't happy with the move. I was a bit nervous, having only really been to Felixstowe Docks but assumed that once I had got used to the new procedures that a new dockyard would require, it would be easy enough. I was right.

On our first day at Seaforth, Eddie and I arrived at the same time. One thing he had been adamant about was not forgetting some form of photo ID as they would not let you in without it. Check. It was easy enough after that. Park up, head into the office, with paperwork and ID, queue up, get more paperwork and a keycard. Walk back to the truck and drive to the security gate, hand over paperwork, get waved on once cleared and stop again so they can check that the security lock (if carrying a loaded container) matches the paperwork. Then the fun begins. Seaforth is a bit of a 'free for all' where trucks are concerned. Unlike Felixstowe, where each driver is assigned a lane and a pad which corresponds to the container they are dropping off or taking away, Seaforth has bays all the way along into which drivers reverse and then, after swiping the keycard on the terminal next to the bay (remember, the card you queued up for earlier?), the information will be passed on to the loaders who will then go and find your container from a big stack and plonk it on you (or lift your box off if you're are delivering). The system is good because if you are dropping off and collecting, it is all done in one transaction whereas at Felixstowe you will be assigned a pad for each transaction, and may even have to drive off to a completely different terminal to collect a box. The only problem with Seaforth's system is that when you enter the loading area, there is a massive queue of lorries at one end and you need to remember which truck was in front of you when you came in through the security gate as you will need to be ready to be next in line after them (or, if it's quiet, who is already parked up in the queue in front of you). Once the lorry in front has left the queue to park in a bay, it is best to pull right forward so no other driver gets the silly idea of jumping the queue. I never saw it happen, most people waited their turn, but I have heard that people have come to blows over queue jumping. Anyway, it pays to be on the ball as the term 'move it or lose it' will be appropriate. Also, if you miss your place in the queue, you are then technically jumping in front of the next person in line which he/she could take offence to as you are then following the person they should be following. I used to write down the registration number of the person in front at the gate and look for them in the queue and wait for them to move.

Very often, I would be given a run south from Liverpool, and then I would have to call in at either Tilbury or Southampton to collect a box going north. I quite enjoyed driving down to Southampton but, on a Friday, it seemed like you would never get there.

My first visit to Southampton docks was a bit of a shambles. No one tells you how it works or what to do and where to go, you just have to find out for yourself or hope you can catch another driver that knows the score. I had a loaded box on which was to be delivered to Pentalver's yard within the docks. I headed south and arrived at the docks, spying Pentalver's yard just inside the entrance. There was quite a queue so I settled in for the wait. Roy from the office phoned me and gave me my PIN number which I would need for picking up my loaded box for the return journey. I took a note of this and settled back into my wait. When I eventually got to the front of the queue, after about half an hour's wait, the lad in the office informed me that this yard was for empty containers only, the yard for loaded containers was at the other end of the docks. Oh well.

Once my container was finally lifted off (another 20 minute wait) I found my way to where I needed to enter my PIN number for my next box. I entered the PIN into the machine but it came up as 'Not Valid'. Hmm, I tried again. No joy. I pressed the intercom and spoke to the security guard and he told me that the number is only valid for 30 minutes and, to gain entry, I would need to speak to my office and obtain another one. I phoned Roy and told him my predicament to which he moaned "Why didn't you tell me you were held up? These numbers cost £25 a time!" No one had told me that. Anyway, he got me another number and I gained entry and loaded my container for the return journey.

I only ever went to Tilbury docks on a couple of occasions so can't really remember the booking in procedure, though I do remember it being quite quick, but that might have just been luck on my part. They give you a number and you sit and wait for it to appear on a big LED screen mounted on the wall of the office building. I wonder how many drivers have fallen asleep and missed their slot?

I would be happy to do any amount of hours from Monday to Friday (within the law), as long as I could be home at a reasonable time on a Friday evening, roughly 5 or 6pm. Roy in the office was quite happy to accommodate me on this and would often phone up during the week asking for something extra and saying "...I haven't forgotten you need an early finish on Friday..." It worked out well for both of us. One Friday morning, after dropping my empty container off at their yard in Gorton, I was given an empty 40ft box to load which I was to take over to Flint in North Wales which they were going to load with a JCB. I arrived and reversed into the yard. This was what I wanted for a Friday, a nice simple job, load up, shut the doors and head for home. I would then take the container to Felixstowe on the Monday morning. Nice, as that would also (usually) get me a box northwards out of Felixstowe and I would get home on the Monday night too. I was spending a lot of nights out in the lorry around this time, which was pretty boring, so any chance of sleeping in my own bed was welcomed.

I opened the rear doors and the lads in the yard trundled over with the machine. Drive on, secure it, shut the doors. Easy. I spoke too soon! The bloody thing wouldn't fit, it was too high. After ages of faffing about, they realised they should have ordered a hi-cube box instead of the standard size I was sat with. I phoned Roy and explained the situation and he told me to return the empty to Seaforth and collect a loaded box for Nottingham for the Monday morning and he would send out another driver with a hi-cube to collect the JCB. This was not what I wanted to hear. The time was now 1pm and, though that still sounds early, traffic would be building all the way round Manchester, and the trucks would all be queuing at Seaforth. So much for my early finish. That's the problem with driving for a living, there is no way you can plan anything, there are too many variables.

One day, at Seaforth, when my box had been lifted off, I noticed that one of my twist locks was loose. The handle had come away from the body so it could easily fall off in the road. I re-secured it as best I could and thought nothing more of it. Later that day, all four twist locks were still present when I unlocked them to have the container lifted off. Once the container had been removed, the lock was nowhere to be seen. It must have still been attached to the bottom of the container. Shit! I phoned my boss back in Nottingham, and he told me to load a box for the morning and he would sort it out later that day once I returned to the yard which, illegally, they didn't have so you'll have to read that as 'industrial estate round the corner from where they were hoping to buy a yard'. Actually, they did eventually buy a yard locally, I think I parked in there a total of once. I honestly don't think it was big enough for 4 lorries plus trailers. Still, it kept them right in the eyes of the law, I suppose. I returned that day and spoke to my boss on the phone to remind him to fix the twist lock.

The next morning, on arriving at my lorry and carrying out my daily checks, I noted the lock was still missing. It was very early and I was due to deliver this box to the Rail Freight Terminal at Old Trafford. I headed north on the M1 and west on the M62. I knew my way here, having been a couple of times in the past. My box was lifted off and I was instructed to move forwards a few truck lengths so they could re-load me. I waited a few minutes before the crane rumbled up with my new box, bound for Bury. The loader was about to lower the container, when he stopped and beeped his horn. I jumped out of the cab and headed round to see what the problem was. He called down saying he wouldn't load me with only 3 twist locks. Good for him.

I phoned my boss (bearing in mind it was still 5am) and he said to wait and that he would call me back in a bit. As soon as I had put the phone down (or pressed the off button as it was a mobile), Eddie phoned. He was stuck at the industrial estate and wasn't going anywhere. He had parked up and gone home for the night and, on arriving back that morning and checking his trailer, he found that both rear light lenses were missing, someone had stolen them. The only suspects were the dodgy company that also parked in the road (despite having a huge yard) and used to get shirty with us for parking in 'their' road. Eddie was not going anywhere and would have to wait until new lenses were found. We had a good laugh about both of our predicaments, and hung up. My phone rang again and it was my boss. He was now livid that I had been on the phone to someone else. I told him Eddie had phoned. He obviously knew that each one of us knew about the other's problems and went up the wall!! "I'M YOUR BOSS, YOU ONLY SPEAK TO ME!!!" he bellowed. Ha, ha, I just found it funny. He then calmed down and gave me directions to a nearby place that would be able to fit a new twist lock, where I headed to and got a replacement fitted on. This all took, including waiting time/travelling time/fixing time, about 3 hours to get sorted. Meanwhile, the container was late leaving the depot, late to be delivered, and it had cost my company in wages and fuel. If my boss had sorted the problem out at the yard the night before, none of this would have been an issue. If we didn't have to park in the street, Eddie's lights probably wouldn't have got nicked either. Incidentally, I think he got the whole day off work with that one as replacements weren't found until late in the day.

It's probably a bit unkind to call the company from our industrial estate dodgy, and suspect them of nicking light lenses, but I do have my reasons. They are a well-known haulage company in Mansfield, also renowned for expecting drivers to exceed their legal hours and drive overloaded. I had first-hand experience of this back when I started out driving vans. The agency sent me there one morning for multi-drop work. I arrived and they gave me the keys to an old 3.5 transit van, which I parked up on the bay for loading. The warehouse lads proceeded to load me and, when I asked what the weight was (as I had seen pallets and God knows what being hauled on), they shrugged and said "There's plenty more yet" pointing at a stack of parcels still to be loaded. I collected all the paperwork from the office and headed out onto the road. The vehicle handling didn't feel right, but I put this down to the age of the vehicle and the fact it was probably a bit knackered.

Drop 1 was on the same industrial estate so I managed that one with no problem. My next drops were about 4 miles away so I turned right onto the main road and up the hill. I say 'hill', it was little more than a slight slope. Regardless of this, the van really struggled to make the grade, even in first gear, and was leaving a worrying trail of black smoke belching out behind. This was around 8am and the Nottingham bound traffic was impatiently building up behind me. Sod this, I thought, and turned round at the next available opportunity, and drove straight back to the yard. Needless to say, the bloke in the office was quite surprised to see me. I handed him the keys, told him that if they wanted to overload a driver then they should find someone else to do it.

He jumped up, saying that they could transfer it all onto another, newer, vehicle, pointing to 2 new Sprinter vans across the yard. I walked out, telling them they should have loaded it onto those vehicles to start with instead of trying to take me for a mug. I jumped in my car and left for home, but not before phoning the agency to tell them I had walked off the job and EXACTLY why I had walked off the job. The agency didn't pay me for the hour or so of work I did that morning which I took as them condoning the actions of this haulage company. I didn't work for either again.

Eddie was not happy with what the job had become. He had less nights out than me but that was still too many for him. He only thought he should be delivering one container a day, but that's just not possible. My thoughts were that if you are 'out all week' (i.e. sleeping in your cab from Monday to Thursday), then it doesn't really matter whether you park up at 4 o'clock at night, or 9 o'clock. On one occasion we both parked up at our base for the night at the same time, where our boss had met us with our wages. Eddie had ripped into him then about the hours and nights out so I knew he probably wouldn't be staying around for long.

I had parked up in a layby for the night loaded with tyres for Pirelli in Coventry. Eddie was loaded with the same and we both arrived at Coventry around the same time. We both got unloaded and phoned Roy to see what we were doing next. The instructions came back – head empty up to Tetley's in Leeds, load with beer, and head to Seaforth to get the box taken off. Easy enough. Off we went, I followed him all the way there. Eddie got loaded before me and set off for Liverpool, thinking that he'd get in and out of the docks and home at a reasonable time. I then got loaded and was just passing Birch services when my phone rang. It was one of the other lads from the office asking if I wouldn't mind, once my loaded box was lifted off, getting another empty and heading back to Leeds for another load. I wouldn't need to get back to the docks that night, the next morning would do, but it needed to be loaded and away from Tetley's. No problem, it was still early, plenty of time.

My phone rang a second time. It was Eddie. "I've quit". He was asked the same and refused to do it. He said he would get the loaded box lifted off then head home and park up for the final time. When Eddie started, the job had been pretty easy and I remember him saying that he'd had two nights out in the 3 months he had been there. All of a sudden, he was being made to work and have nights out. I didn't really want nights out and would rather not have been out all week, but that was the job. Take it or leave it. He left it. We were on £430 a week 'take home' regardless of whether we had nights out and regardless of how many hours we worked. He must have weighed it up and decided it wasn't worth it. The problem was, there was nowhere better to work round our neck of the woods. He wouldn't have wanted to go back to the steel delivery company, and the money wouldn't have been as good either. Me? I had never earned so much so stuck with it!

Incidentally, I got my second load from Tetley's in Leeds and still managed to be parked up at Birch services for 6.30 that evening. Was that really worth leaving over?

One Thursday afternoon, once I had dropped my loaded box at Seaforth, I was instructed to head over to Gorton to pick up an empty box from the yard. I was then to head to Knutsford in Cheshire. I arrived in Knutsford and located the industrial estate where I was due first thing the following morning and parked up outside the gates for the night behind another container lorry, three more then parked behind me.

The next morning, we were all told to park in the yard across the road where we would be loaded with machinery for Dortmund in Germany. This company was renewing all their old machines and a company in Dortmund had bought them to, presumably, fix up.

The first truck got loaded, after what seemed like ages. The container was full of old lathes, all slotted in, with all their various auxiliary parts secured to the correct machine. The driver then took his paperwork and disappeared. I was in next to load and it was the same again, lots of faffing about and lots of securing with chains and ratchet straps. Still, I thought, it was quite early. If I could be loaded and away for about 11, I'd be in with a good chance of getting home at a reasonable time. My trailer was due back for an inspection and service over the weekend, so I was heading back 'skelly only' which meant not too much hanging around when I dropped this load back to Gorton. I was eventually loaded and handed my paperwork. I proceeded to drive out of the yard but, before I could make it, a small guy with glasses and a beard jumped in front of me shouting "STOP!!" I slammed on the brakes and he came round to my window explaining (in a German accent) that I have the wrong paperwork for my load. Actually, what he meant was that he would have to open up the container and change the identification plates on all the machines as it is illegal to ship them with the old numbers as the paperwork didn't match. I assumed he knew what he was doing and left him too it. This process took another 2 hours as half of the machines had to be removed and reloaded so that he could reach those at the front of the load. I did chuckle though as I thought about the first truck which was probably already at the docks. I'm not sure if he got called back or whether the machines ended up stuck at German customs with a heavy fine.

Once he was satisfied, I was allowed to leave. I still got back to the Gorton container yard in good time and, not having to load, was away and clear of the Manchester ring road at 3.30pm which meant I'd be home for about half past 5. I had just turned onto the A628 when the phone rang but I didn't answer it as I could say that I had no phone reception across this part of the moors.

On Monday morning, when I arrived back at Gorton, Roy told me that he had tried to phone me on Friday afternoon as they needed one more container back at Knutsford. It paid not to answer the phone as I'd either have had to refuse the load (and that gets you in trouble and would probably put an end to my Friday finishes in future) or I would have had to go back to Gorton to collect a container, head to Knutsford to load (through rush hour) wait 2 or 3 hours to actually get loaded, and back to Gorton to get the container taken off. I'd be lucky to have been home before midnight!

I have never been one for driving illegally or exceeding my driving or working hours and I always take my breaks when I should. I know some drivers that lose their tacho charts, or pull the tachograph fuse (so it doesn't register everything). Some drivers even have a switch for this purpose, otherwise known as a 'wire', so they can turn it on or off when they please. Highly illegal. I will, very rarely, bend the rules slightly if it will make my life easier.

On one occasion, Roy phoned me to ask if I could load in Southampton for Nottingham. The delivery was due at midnight but, seeing as I had loaded at lunch time, I arrived at the drop around 6pm. I drove up to the security gate, hoping I would get a quick tip as I had to get the empty back down to Southampton and reload the next day, a Friday. I figured I could get unloaded and use the last hour of my driving time to get a bit further south before parking up. I would then have my 9 hours daily rest before heading off first thing in the morning. This should get me into, and out of, Southampton docks in good time to beat the rush and home at a reasonable time for a Friday. The security guard had other ideas.

He was about to let me through the gate when he noticed the delivery time on my paperwork. "You can park round the corner until your allotted time". Damn! That's scuppered my plan. I parked round the corner and removed my tacho chart. This meant I was now on my 9 hour break so couldn't move. Only, I had to get on the bay at the depot round the corner. Also, when I had parked up, the little cul-de-sac was empty so I parked right at the bottom. There was a little hall about halfway down which obviously had some sort of function on as the car park, then road, started to fill with cars (some badly parked). To top it all off, a couple of lorries came down to park up. I decided that I could very easily get blocked in as there wasn't much room to manoeuvre so I headed for the start of the cul-de-sac and parked up where I could easily get out. I had already eaten and tried to get some sleep but was unable to as there was too much movement going on.

My delivery time was nearing so I headed back round to the security gate and was directed to a bay. I opened the back doors and reversed onto the bay. I pulled the blinds down and managed some broken sleep between the blaring radio and the violent rocking motion of my trailer being unloaded. Once I was clear, I pulled out of the yard and back round the corner and waited until my 9 hours rest was up, meanwhile drinking some strong black coffee. I was now 'legal' to drive again, in the eyes of the tacho, but not in the eyes of the law. I proceeded to head south to Southampton.

On the northbound dual carriageway near the docks, just off a roundabout, there is quite a sharp bend in the road. Halfway round the bend was a container lorry lying on its side. Maybe the camber caught the driver out? Maybe he was driving too fast for the bend (unlikely, as it was uphill in their direction of travel and straight off a roundabout so unlikely they would manage to get a great deal of speed up)? Maybe the container was badly loaded? Maybe the driver hadn't had his full rest the night before, or had exceeded his driving hours? A lesson to us all, it made me think and I have never done it again. One slip or lack of concentration can mean damage or death.

One of the drivers at the dialysis company had a bad

accident whilst I worked there. He was driving round a left hand bend when he lost control, smashed through a wall, crashed through a BMW dealership damaging 6 brand new cars, through another wall before ending up with the vehicle on its side in a field. He claimed that the sun got in his eyes. My transport manager, whilst telling me the story, said "That's probably what I'd have said, too" in that knowing way only an ex-trucker could.

Another very experienced driver I knew was driving an artic pulling an empty flatbed trailer one night when a ratchet strap, which was just resting on the walkway behind the cab rather than being neatly stowed away in the purpose built 'strap box', unravelled itself and got caught round the prop. Had the vehicle been loaded, the torque would have probably snapped it but, instead, the wheels of the unit jammed up causing the trailer to jack-knife and the whole rig ended up in a field, narrowly missing a house.

Thankfully, no-one was injured in the above accidents, but it just goes to show how these concentration lapses can catch up with even the most experienced of drivers.

EXHAUST GAS

I want to say a few words about something very important here. Now, on the roads and in the truck stops, drivers' canteens and transport offices up and down the country, there are many, many stories of the road. Some, like the ones above, are true. Others, like the toilet seat hanging from the back of the trailer, probably aren't. Though it's probably not true that there's a truck somewhere with a bog seat hanging off it, it is true that I was told that story, if you see what I mean?

It's time to meet an old friend, he's called the 'truckers myth'. This will be told to you by someone you work with, and you may or may not believe them, but you probably will.

I was told a story once about a trucker from Nottingham that was driving in Spain. He phoned his boss and said "I have a problem, my driver's side mirror is broken".

"Well, you have Scania response throughout Europe, give them a call and they'll sort it out", replied the boss.

To which the driver replied "The only problem is that the truck is lying on it".

Whether you believe that or not is up to you. I did

when I was told. The guy telling me was pretty trustworthy so I had no reason to disbelieve him. Then again, this was the same guy that took a week off work with flu. On his return, he said that one of the office staff had phoned him to see if he was fit for work on the Monday and if he felt better. He told them he was and would be back, no problem. He then told me he was actually sat on a beach in Corfu when the phone rang. Maybe he isn't the most trustworthy of people after all.

Anyway, I moved away to Scotland some years later and started working for a new firm. I got chatting to some of the lads and I told them the story of the driver in Spain with his mirror, starting with "I know someone who had a mate that was driving in Spain….." which (I thought) was true. It was a couple of weeks later when a couple of the other drivers and I had to go to the garage to pick up our trucks as they had been in for a service. Blow me if one of them didn't tell the story, starting with "A mate of mine was in Spain…." It then dawned on me that this story has probably spread like wildfire for years before I had heard it. It was rather strange having it regurgitated back to me in that manner.

A BIT DEFLATED

I arrived at Seaforth Docks one sunny afternoon and parked up. I was about midway in the queue when another driver I had spoken to in the past came over for a chat. We were probably having a good moan about the docks when I noticed my near side front tyre was looking a bit flat. I was loathe to leave the queue as it would mean I'd have to go to the back, but there was no way I could leave it like it was. I found out from a couple of drivers that there was a small garage within the grounds of the docks that would be able to blow the tyre up for me. I got directions and found the garage and one of the mechanics kindly let me use his air compressor. I went back to the queue and managed to get back to the position I was before.

I eventually got loaded with a box for Pirelli in Coventry. I liked this as I knew where I was going, having delivered there a few times over the past month. My driving hours were running short for the day so I pulled in to Lymm truck stop for the night, filling the tanks with diesel before parking up. I had kept an eye on the tyre and it was looking flat again so I phoned my boss and asked him to get a tyre fitter out that night to get a new one on. He wasn't happy as the deflating tyre was quite new and still had a lot of tread left on it but it wouldn't stay up, so something had to be done.

I got a phone call from the tyre fitter about an hour later saying that he was very busy and wouldn't be able to get to me until around midnight. I had eaten and decided I'd watch a DVD before trying to get a bit of sleep before he arrived. There was a knock on my door just before midnight which woke me from my restless sleep and I could tell it was the tyre fitter by the orange strobe lights that I could see flickering through the curtains. He jacked the cab up and started up his compressor. Now, I don't know if you have heard how loud a compressor is? During the day the noise gets lost but at night, in a quiet truck stop, when you know that every driver around you is asleep, the noise is deafening! Then, to add insult to injury, he starts removing the wheel nuts with the compressor tool which sounds like a machine gun bursting into life and echoing round the whole lorry park. There is no quiet way to do this and I apologise to all the other drivers that were there that night. The tyre was changed in good time (thankfully) and I got back into my bed without getting punched by an irate, half asleep, trucker (thankfully).

The next morning, the tyre was still up, and, after checking that no irate, half-asleep trucker had pulled my 5th wheel pin (which would cause my trailer to crash down onto its knees when I pulled away), I headed for Coventry. By the time I arrived, the tyre was half deflated again. This was getting tedious. There was another lorry getting unloaded so I headed back onto the motorway to get some air at Corley Services. My boss had asked if I could try and get the lorry back to the yard so he could get the tyre fixed without paying for another call out. This wasn't to be, though, as it was nearly flat when I arrived back at Pirelli's. I reversed onto the bay for unloading and, not long after, another tyre fitter arrived and removed the tyre. He thought that the wheel looked like it might be the culprit so changed it and put the same tyre back on. By the time he was done, my lorry was empty, so I headed back to the yard, checking the tyre a few times on the journey back and it had thankfully stayed up this time. The only problem now was that there was a perfectly good tyre sat in the back of a tyre fitters somewhere in Runcorn. It would probably be worth a few hundred quid and my boss didn't stop reminding me to collect it "if I was empty and passing". I never seemed to be either passing or empty and it was a few months later when I decided I'd make a special trip to collect it and bung it in the cab. The fitters were true to their word and, after a bit of a search, found the tyre under a pile of other tyres in their shed.

A LOT LIZARD?

You'll hear a lot of talk about 'ladies of the night' or, as they say in America, 'lot lizards'. You'll hear stories of drivers being woken in the middle of the night by a tap on the door, or getting 'propositioned' in a layby by a scantily clad maiden. In all the years I have been driving, and parking up in different locations, I have never encountered one, very sorry to disappoint you! I'm not saying that some of these stories aren't true, but I personally wouldn't believe them all.

I was delivering in Manchester one day and had just driven under the arches at Piccadilly Station when my phone rang. I needed to speak to the transport office so pulled into a side street. There was nowhere to park a lorry so I headed to the bottom of the cul-de-sac and managed to park on a small patch of waste ground. The phone had, by now, stopped ringing so I dialled the number and waited. The transport manager answered and I started chatting to him. In the corner of my eye, I was aware of someone walking in my direction, but I didn't pay much attention to them. As they got closer, I looked up to see a prostitute rapidly advancing towards me. Then, as if by magic, a police car also appeared from the same direction I had come from. SHIT! The woman seemed unaware (or didn't care) that the police had just arrived. Me, on the other hand, was by now jumping up and down in my seat and trying to convey the 'no, it's ok, I'm good thanks and I don't require your services' in hand gestures, whilst still trying to maintain a conversation on the phone without letting on what was happening. She kept moving towards the truck. I locked both doors and ignored her. Thankfully the police turned round and headed off, obviously having more important things to do. Phew, that could have been awkward to explain away. "So, tell me again, what are you doing in a known red light area of Manchester, talking to a prostitute?"

I pulled into Hilton Park services one sunny afternoon, fresh from a day of delivering to Birmingham. I was doing well for time and pulled in for my last 15 minute break (this is before the new law that states the last break of the 45 minutes must be at least 30 minutes, back then you could take a 15 and 30 minute, a 30 and 15 minute, or 3 x 15 minute breaks or even a 20 and 25 minute break). No sooner had I parked up when a lady, smiling sweetly at me, walked round to the passenger side of my cab. Before I had time to react, she was in. Thoughts flashed through my mind of police cars screeching round the corner, and arresting me without a word. In court, I would protest but couldn't really deny I had been caught red-handed! Luckily, it turned out, there were a few of these ladies working that day and they were asking drivers to fill out a questionnaire regarding our health and personal insurance cover. When you think about it, it's a bit of a dodgy occupation for a lone female, hanging around a lorry park and jumping into any old drivers' cab, whether she's working legally or illegally.

Another disease of the service station is the 'mobile retailer'. These aren't the friendly Hot Dog wagon or ice cream truck. No, these are men, usually, that drive round looking for unsuspecting patrons to buy their dodgy goods. I've been offered everything from gold watches to leather jackets and I wouldn't touch any of them with a barge pole. They usually come up with a story like "I am from Italy and we have just attended an exhibition where we were showing our beautiful leather jackets. We don't want to ship them home as it will cost too much, so we wondered if you would like to buy one at a bargain price?" No thank you. Another tried the line "I am a local retailer, I have some excess stock due to an over order, we don't have room in our shop, so I was wondering if you would like to bag a bargain?". The same guy tried this on me at Hartshead Moor Services and London Gateway Services, and screeched off rather rapidly when I asked how local his shop was as I'd seen him in Yorkshire two days before?!

TWISTING THE TRUTH

A lot of lies and/or exaggeration can be heard in the driver's canteen but, more often than you should (and more than is professional) you'll hear it from your own transport office. You may well be told to "Just tell them that...." when late arriving with a delivery. I never would.

I had just delivered a load of steel to a building site in Leicester when the phone rang. "Could you head up to the 'painters' and load a girder for the new Coventry stadium?" The 'painters', based just outside Ilkeston, was just that, and we would often get a nice, freshly painted bit of steelwork loaded which would need careful strapping down so as not to damage it. "The only problem is, we actually forgot the load should have been delivered first thing today, so just tell them something like, oh I don't know, you overslept this morning".

On arrival at the painters, I got questioned as to why I was late, to which I replied "Sorry mate, I was delivering in Leicester this morning and only got told to come 'ere an hour ago". I'm not lying and making myself look slack, just to make my company look good.

On another occasion, I turned up with a load to the Coventry stadium (again, from the painters) and the foreman enquired if I had managed to get my batteries sorted out. It was the first I had heard about it, the company obviously lying on my behalf as they had (again) forgotten that a load was needed that day!

Another day found me at Tilbury Docks, loading a 20ft container full of beans for Selby. My legal driving hours were nearly up so I found a layby on the A13 to park up in for the night, just before hitting the M25. The layby was not ideal, being one of those where there is nothing between the vehicle and the dual carriageway. I would much rather have some form of barrier or grassy verge in the way as you'll get a better nights' sleep away from the main road as every passing vehicle rocks the cab, and, more importantly, it's a lot safer. I once saw the aftermath of an accident on the A14, just before the M11 split. I was heading eastbound and saw a truck parked in a layby on the other carriageway. The whole front of the truck was just a mangled mess, horrific stuff. Judging by the time of morning, the driver was probably in his bed and, seeing as there was no way he could have survived that (unless a miracle happened and he'd jumped out for a piss at exactly the right moment) one can just hope he didn't feel a thing. It was hard to see what had happened but, on closer inspection, the rear end of another truck was off to the side, through a fence, and sitting in someone's back garden. He'd either fallen asleep or lost concentration, and left the road, wiping out the truck cab and fence in his wake. Scary stuff, so I always try to park up in a decent layby where I can.

Once parked up, I phoned my boss to tell him that I was out of hours for the day and would set off first thing in the morning (reducing my daily rest to 9 hours) and would arrive in Selby at approximately midday. I was booked in for 9am, so best to let them know that I'll be late.

On arriving at the delivery point in Selby, three blokes were waiting in a white van, having a smoke. As soon as I pulled in, they came racing over. "You were supposed to be here 3 hours ago!" one shouted. I protested, telling them that there was no way I was going to get here at that time, and I had told my boss who should have passed on the message. He obviously hadn't, so I got the blame. They calmed down and unloaded the container by hand in double-quick time as they were booked in to unload another truck in half an hours' time for another company just down the road. This is all they did all day, driving round various companies and 'handballing' loads out of containers. If they had have known I'd be late, they could have arranged to be somewhere else instead of sitting around, waiting for me.

A BAD DAY

I had loaded in Southampton on the Friday, with a load for Oldham. The 40ft container was loaded with leather jackets so I parked up as safely as I could that night and padlocked the rear doors before going home for the weekend.

Monday morning came and I started the engine of my Renault Magnum, filled out a new tachograph chart, stowed away the weeks' clothes and food and did my walk round checks of my unit and trailer, giving the tyres a kick, checking the tread and also checking the lights were working. My lorry had developed an annoying habit in which the brake lights stuck on. Nothing would turn them off so, when I parked up for long periods, I would have to turn the isolator switch off. This was located on the nearside of the unit, just next to the fuel tank, and it shut down the electrics to everything. This was equally annoying and dangerous. If I parked up in a layby for the night, which I did regularly, it meant that last thing at night, I would have to clamber out of my cab (sometimes freezing cold, sometimes raining) and switch it off. The Magnum had electric blinds instead of curtains so they would have to be closed before isolating the battery. If anything happened in the night, like some dodgy sorts coming into the layby, possibly to steal my load, I'd be unable to drive off without exiting the cab first. It also meant that my brake lights didn't work, as they were always on. This was an intermittent fault, so for a good portion of the time, they did work but that's not good enough, they should work all the time. I had told my boss about this fault numerous times, the unit even passed its MOT test without them being fixed. They obviously didn't play up on that occasion. My cab had also developed a slight lean on the drivers' side. It looked like the suspension was lower so there must have been a problem there, too. With hindsight, I should have told him that I wouldn't be driving it again until it was fixed. I was a new driver at the time though, and would probably have been out of a job if he took the lorry off the road as he didn't have a replacement. I still didn't even have a year of Class 1 driving experience so certainly didn't fit within the 2 year minimum that most companies require. These problems, very soon, were not going to be an issue though......

I set off on the A38 and headed north on the M1. Traffic was getting heavy, but still flowing at a good speed. I put a CD in the player and sat back and relaxed into the journey. I had delivered to this warehouse in Oldham before so knew exactly where I was going.

I got to about 5 miles from the Lofthouse interchange, where the M1 and M62 meet, when the traffic started getting heavier. Nothing unusual for this time of day, especially on a Monday morning. The weather had started out clear and, though the sun was still shining, the road was slightly wet. I had just passed junction 41 when everything ahead came to a halt. The usual stop/start with cars trying to enter the motorway from the slip road as well as vehicles moving over to lane 1 from lane 2 to turn off onto the M62, a mile or so ahead. Everything started to move again and I was now only yards away from the M62 slip road. This time, when everything came to a stop, it was more abrupt.

Everything that occurred next seemed to happen in slow motion. I was fully aware that the lorry in front had stopped, but I was also aware that I wasn't going to stop in time and that I would eventually stop about 3 feet in front of his trailer doors.

I looked round in a daze. The windscreen was shattered, all my personal belongings were everywhere in the cab, blue smoke was rising from somewhere. My knees hurt. This was one mess I couldn't get out of without anyone noticing. I sat in my cab for what seemed like an hour. The truck in front eventually peeled itself away from the front of mine. Two men, I assumed from vehicles ahead, were sat on the barrier by the hard shoulder, making no attempt to help me out. The traffic on the motorway had slowed at first but was now back to whizzing past. Life went on. I couldn't open my door. The Renault Magnum cab is designed so that the top part of the cab (where the driver sits) moves independently from the bottom of the cab (where the wheels and engine are located). The impact had left the top part of the cab out of alignment with the bottom, so the door was getting caught on the chassis. The only way to open it was with a kick, but that's a risky thing to do with traffic hurtling past, only inches away.

I could now see the police had arrived on the scene. I had managed to open my door and looked round for my phone. It was kept in a cubby-hole on the dashboard, just to the left of the steering wheel, but nothing was recognisable as the dash had collapsed and the cubby-hole was nowhere to be seen. I felt around on the floor and found my phone and exited the cab, heading to the safety of the hard shoulder.

A policeman greeted me there with a breathalyser; standard procedure. I passed that, as I knew I would. Looking round, things looked a bit clearer. The truck in front of me had ploughed into the rear of a van. That's why it stopped so abruptly. The van had pulled in from lane 2 to lane 1, slamming its brakes on. Trucks take longer to stop, so the poor guy in front had no chance. There didn't seem to be too much damage to either vehicle. I then hit the back of the lorry. In doing so, I had stopped quickly, causing a car behind me to crash in the back of my trailer. I didn't even know this had happened until I was looking at the whole scene. The car driver was also changing from lane 2 to 1 when I suddenly stopped. What a mess!

I could see a patch of black oil underneath my truck; not a good sign. The policeman asked me if I was able to move it so the motorway could be made safe. I got back into the cab and reached for the gear stick to check it was in neutral, but couldn't find it. The impact had caused it to drop down to an odd position, probably because the gear box, or connecting rods, were now out of alignment. I turned the key to start the engine. Instead of starting, it just made a horrid grinding noise and, according to one of the other drivers, oil was pouring out underneath as I did so. We were going nowhere. All the other vehicles were on the hard shoulder by now, mine had come off the worst out of all of them (though the car behind me was probably a write-off, it was still moveable).

The police radioed for a tow truck, which arrived a short while later. I had also phoned my boss to tell him the bad news. He was OK about it, his first questions asking if I was alright, and if anyone else was hurt. Thankfully no one was. My knees were hurting where they impacted the dashboard, but it was nothing worth worrying about.

The tow truck moved my lorry onto the hard shoulder and, after swapping details with the police and other drivers, I got into the cab and was taken to the salvage company's yard, a few miles up the road in Dewsbury. My boss was on his way to pick me up and take me home and all I could do was clear my cab out. That was a strange thing, trying to locate everything. I used to keep things on the top bunk as it had a large dip in the middle so, I assumed, it would hold things in the event of braking sharply. It didn't. I think my one-ring cooker hit the windscreen with enough force to crack the glass. I have seen many truck drivers with their children in the cab, clambering around, not strapped into their seat and it doesn't bear thinking about what the damage would look like in the event of an accident.

My boss arrived and helped me get the rest of my gear out of the cab and into his car. He had a look round and seemed more annoyed that the fuel tanks were nearly full (about 700 litres) which the insurance company wouldn't let him syphon out. They wouldn't let him remove the CD player either, or the good tyres, everything had to remain as it was and they would pay out on that basis.

On the journey home he explained that he didn't have another vehicle to use on container work, which I knew already, but there was a nightshift run to Scotland 5 nights a week that I could do, starting that night. No thanks. I had been up since 5am, managed to have an accident, and he wanted me to jump in a lorry that night and drive to Scotland and back? He said that I should get back in the driving seat as soon as possible, which was fair enough, but I didn't think it would be a good idea to be that night. He also kept asking if I had been distracted, was I on the phone etc. "It's OK you can tell me, I just want to know what happened". Yeah right. I had not been on the phone, or distracted, or anything else. A couple of his other drivers phoned him on the journey home to see how I was doing. They both said they'd had bad accidents at some point or another, it's nothing to be ashamed of but I am a self-regulated perfectionist so it was to me! One had tipped a wagon over on a roundabout, ending up crouched in the passenger footwell whilst the lorry slid to a halt on its side. My boss had ended up jack-knifing and crashing into a motorway barrier after a truck pulled out in front of him from a slip road.

In the days and weeks after my accident, I pondered what might have been if....

What would have happened if there was a car between me and the truck in front? It could have been crushed, probably killing the driver. Worse still, it could have been a motorbike.

What if, instead of just a bit of blue smoke, the cab had caught fire? I might not have been able to open the door in time and burned to death.

What if my brake lights were stuck on and the driver behind had reported me to the police, and I was blamed for the whole thing? Thankfully they weren't stuck on at this time.

There are many things that could have happened but thankfully didn't.

You may be thinking "This is what happens when you are travelling too fast and too close to the vehicle in front". In part, you'd be correct, we were all travelling too close to the vehicle in front as, if we weren't, we'd have been able to stop. As for speed, how fast would you have to be going to cause such damage? I checked my tacho chart a few days later and the vehicle speed, at the very moment before it stopped dead, was 27 miles per hour.

THE END OF THE ROAD

Well, it was the end of that particular journey, anyway. It took me quite a while to get over the accident and get things straight in my head. I was back to driving soon afterwards, just not for the same firm. I have had many jobs since, but nothing compares with the early days of driving and the learning curve we all have to go through. Sure, I've had a few scrapes since, most recently reversing into a brand new Portacabin, leaving a 2ft long scrape down the side and knocking it off its concrete base. Not my finest moment, admittedly, but shit happens. Admit to it, take the grief from your colleagues and move on.

Most drivers will tell you that they hate the job, the wages are crap, and the hours are terrible. All drivers moan, it's in our nature to. A lot of drivers change jobs on a regular basis. Even more drivers SAY they will leave their job if they don't get their own way, but rarely actually change. I recently worked with a driver that always claimed "They'll be looking for another driver...." when things didn't go his way, it had almost become a habit. Funnily enough, he quizzed me a few months back about agency wages and vowed that, once his licence had been returned to him (he'd sent it away, along with a medical, to get it renewed), he would be leaving. I have asked him a few times since about when he'll be leaving and, rather strangely, he still hasn't had his licence returned to him. The DVLA really aren't what they used to be……

Printed in Poland
by Amazon Fulfillment
Poland Sp. z o.o., Wrocław